PhilanthropyRoundtable

Catholic School Renaissance

A Wise Giver's Guide to Strengthening a National Asset

By Andy Smarick and Kelly Robson

Published by The Philanthropy Roundtable, 1730 M Street NW, Suite 601, Washington, DC, 20036.

Free copies of this book are available to qualified donors. To learn more, or to order more copies, call (202) 822-8333, e-mail main@PhilanthropyRoundtable.org, or visit PhilanthropyRoundtable.org. Printed and e-book versions are available from major online booksellers. A PDF may be downloaded at no charge at PhilanthropyRoundtable.org.

Cover: © Donna Wells/shutterstock

ISBN 978-0-9861474-3-2
LCCN 2015950783

First printing, October 2015

Current Wise Giver's Guides from The Philanthropy Roundtable

Karl Zinsmeister, *series editor*
For all current and future titles, visit PhilanthropyRoundtable.org/guidebook

TABLE OF CONTENTS

PREFACE

An Encouraging Moment

The Philanthropy Roundtable has been a national leader in school reform for two decades, and every year we deepen our expertise and ability to guide donors who want to invest in improving American schooling. In just the past couple years we've produced five meaty how-to guides outlining practical details of being a savvy donor in various sectors of education reform.

This guidebook on the best ways to support Catholic schools is an all-new successor to our guide published six years ago on the same topic. With research background from Anthony Pienta of the Roundtable, it was written by educational-excellence authority Andy Smarick and Kelly Robson of Bellwether Education Partners. Andy and the editor of this guidebook, Karl Zinsmeister, organized the first White House Summit on Catholic and other faith-based schools back in 2008, where the President released their White House report on the "crisis" in religious schooling, *Preserving a Critical National Asset*.

The present moment is much more encouraging. This new book includes the freshest data and the very latest case histories, and compared to the Roundtable's previous book and the White House report, the prognosis for Catholic schooling looks much brighter. Indeed, we believe these institutions that contribute so much to our nation (and especially to urban families and the health of our cities) could be on the cusp of a renaissance.

It is donors who will mostly decide that. They helped Catholic schools turn a corner over the past few years, and if they step in now with expanded resource support and a burst of energy backing modernization and accountability, some deeply impressive things can happen during the next decade in our Catholic schools.

The Philanthropy Roundtable gratefully acknowledges assistance toward the publication of this guidebook from the Achelis and Bodman, Louis Calder, William E. Simon, and Riordan foundations, and John Stollenwerk.

Adam Meyerson
President, The Philanthropy Roundtable

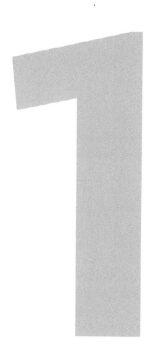

Catholic Schools Are a Good Investment Today

For nearly 50 years, American K–12 Catholic education was in a quiet retreat. Thousands of schools were shuttered. Enrollment plummeted by millions. Though heroic educators and generous donors stemmed the tide in many places, even creating exemplars of what was possible, forecasts were bleak. The threat seemed existential. Education journals carried articles titled, "Can Catholic Schools Be Saved?"

But thanks to an unprecedented wave of social entrepreneurialism and some innovative public policies—both fueled by philanthropy—we may be witnessing a renaissance in Catholic K-12 education. New approaches to organizing, governing, funding, and staffing these schools are showing that this sector can be financially sustainable, in addition to producing terrific student outcomes. Donors of all faiths, and even no faith, are participating—recognizing the valuable things that Catholic schools do for the nation, in particular by educating inner-city children who have been failed by many other sectors. (See the Spring 2010 cover story of *Philanthropy* magazine for reporting on the role of non-Catholic donors in boosting Catholic schools.)

At the end of a roller-coaster ride

America's first Catholic schools were created decades before our nation was even founded. They served millions of needy children, and lifted up waves of impoverished immigrant families. As our urban demographics shifted dramatically during the twentieth century, it was increasingly low-income African-American and Hispanic families who flocked to urban Catholic schools as an alternative to dysfunctional government-run schools. While adjusting to meet the changing needs of their students and communities, Catholic schools continued to provide rigorous, faith-inspired education.

But growing labor costs, rising secularization, the shift of Catholic parishioners to the suburbs, and an increasingly competitive schools landscape pushed Catholic schools to insolvency in many places. While in 1965 more than 13,000 Catholic schools served 5.6 million students, 50 years later there were 6,568 schools serving 1.9 million students.

Catholic educators and donors have responded to these downtrends with determination and creativity, and American K-12 Catholic schooling is now reorganizing to bounce back. A wider range of school operators are inspiring improved funding, governing themselves in more innovative and businesslike ways, creating more pipelines for staffing talent, and producing clearer results. Philanthropic support is broader than ever. Ed Hanway, former chairman of Cigna and longtime Catholic-schools donor, believes "There has never been a better time to invest in Catholic education."

The past is prologue

To understand where Catholic K-12 schooling stands and why its future is brightening, it is helpful to understand its mercurial past.

America's first Catholic school was opened by Franciscan friars in 1606 in present-day St. Augustine, Florida. Throughout the 1600s and 1700s, education in America was regarded mostly as a private matter to be provided by family members, tutors, religious leaders, and others with specific areas of expertise. By the early nineteenth century more formal community schools began to emerge, and the Catholic Church became one provider. As waves of Catholic immigrants arrived from Europe, Catholic schools began to spring up around parish churches.

Catholics represented only one percent of the population during the Revolutionary era, but by 1891 more than one out of eight Americans were Catholic. Cities like New York, Chicago, Boston, Philadelphia, and Cincinnati were awash in Catholic children, most of them poor. By 1900, approximately 3,500 parish schools existed in the U.S. These schools typically took on the character of their communities, emphasizing ethnic culture and native-language instruction.

Responding to the growing demand for Catholic schoolteachers, Elizabeth Seton founded the Sisters of Charity in 1808 to train nuns as educators (see box). In 1852, America's Catholic bishops committed to a large expansion of parochial schools where Catholic children could be taught. By then, and for generations to come, a large majority of the teachers in these schools were women living under religious vows.

At the same time Catholic schools were spreading, states and local governments were developing the nation's early system of public

Catholic School Enrollment

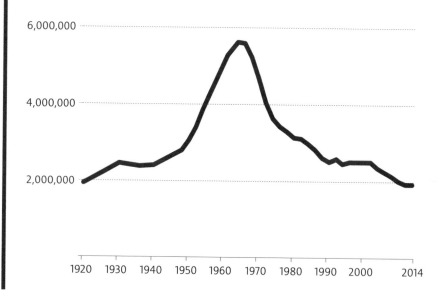

education. By the time Horace Mann became the first secretary of the Massachusetts Board of Education in 1837, "common schools" were proliferating. Though government-run, they were not secular, and their Protestant character ran counter to some Catholic teachings. Many required devotional readings out of the King James Version of the Bible, which was not used by the Catholic Church, and some textbooks had passages disparaging Catholics.

In many cities, Catholic students migrated to schools provided by their church, but by 1875, 14 states had passed laws prohibiting "sectarian" schools from receiving public funds. President Grant gave a speech that year urging that "a good common school education" should be "unmixed with atheistic, pagan, or sectarian tenets." Speaker of the House James Blaine introduced a Constitutional amendment embodying this idea. It was narrowly defeated in the U.S. Senate, but by 1890 "Blaine Amendments" had been added to 29 state constitutions, explicitly prohibiting public funds from going to sectarian schools.

In 1884 the U.S. Catholic bishops took their next step and *required* every Catholic parish to establish a school, and required parents to send their children to it. Although not all parishes complied, Catholic-school enrollment exploded from 405,000 children in 1880 to 1.9 million

Number of Catholic Schools

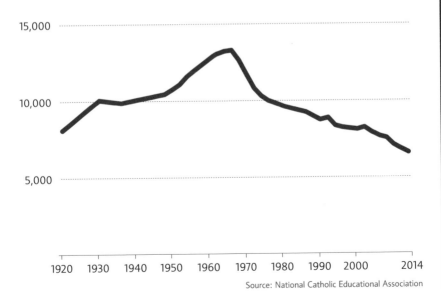

Source: National Catholic Educational Association

in 1920. The landmark 1925 Supreme Court decision *Pierce v. Society of Sisters* upheld the right of parents to send their children to private schools, and declared state requirements that students must attend public schools to be un-Constitutional. Catholic-school enrollment grew rapidly over the next decades.

The post-World War II Baby Boom accelerated this growth. The number of children in Catholic K–12 schools peaked at 5.6 million (attending 13,000 schools) during the 1965-66 school year. This represented 12 percent of all the schoolchildren in the U.S., and 87 percent of the students outside of government-run schools.

Then change roared across the nation. White Catholic families departed cities in droves. Church membership and Catholic observance declined, and the flow of new nuns and priests shrunk to a trickle. With anti-Catholic bigotry having evaporated (the nation elected its first Catholic President in 1960), fewer parents felt the need to shelter their children in Catholic schools. Between 1966 and 2014, the number of Catholic schools tumbled from 13,292 to 6,568.

Since they were financed primarily through parishioners' tithes and the donated labor of nuns and priests, Catholic schools had been nearly free. As parishioners and vocational volunteers disappeared, however, so did the income stream of these schools. With the proportion of the teaching staff under religious vows having dropped to just 7 percent by 2000, the cost of hiring lay teachers brought soaring financial demands on parishes.

Meanwhile, charter schools, first opening in the early 1990s, created further enrollment losses for urban Catholic schools. Charters are public schools that receive government funding, along with philanthropic support, and are therefore tuition-free. In many cities, charters occupy the same ecological role as Catholic schools—a safer, character-based, higher-quality alternative to the neighborhood's assigned public school. Except charters are free to those who attend them. Together, these factors produced dramatic Catholic-school enrollment declines. Between 2004 and 2014, 1,856 Catholic schools were closed or consolidated—a 23 percent loss. Thousands of Catholic schools continue to provide vital services. Continuing challenges, however, threaten their sustainability.

Recruiting, training, and retaining highly effective Catholic-school educators is a perennial concern, especially given the lower salaries at Catholic schools compared to nearby public schools. Many Catholic

Elizabeth Seton, mother of Catholic teachers

Born in 1774, Elizabeth Bayley grew up in a prominent Episcopal family in New York City. At 19, she married wealthy businessman William Seton, and they had five children and enjoyed a prominent social life. Bankruptcy and the death of her husband jolted the course of Elizabeth's life, however, ultimately leading her to a deep devotion to the Catholic faith and a lifetime of serving the poor.

In order to support herself and her children, Elizabeth opened an academy for young ladies. After her conversion to Catholicism Elizabeth accepted a teaching position at St. Mary's College in Baltimore. In 1809 she became a nun.

Then she started a Maryland school dedicated to the education of Catholic girls, and founded an order of religious sisters who helped her establish free schools across the eastern seaboard. Thus began the ministry of Catholic women in America devoted to educating children.

Though Mother Seton died in 1821, her religious sisters continued to bring schools and orphanages to places like Cincinnati and New Orleans, and they established the first hospital west of the Mississippi River in St. Louis. Seton was canonized in 1975 for her role in pioneering U.S. Catholic education, making her the first native-born American to be recognized as a saint by her church. A number of institutions and initiatives honor her name, including Seton Hall University, many churches, and Seton Education Partners, a nonprofit helping to revitalize Catholic schools through technology and blended learning.

schools have had weak and unimaginative financial management. Some old-line Catholic educators have resisted sharing performance data, ignored improved methods of school operation and governance, and neglected innovation. This has inhibited the sector's ability to adapt to a constantly changing and increasingly competitive K–12 landscape.

In the past decade, however, a growing number of bishops, priests, school leaders, teachers, and donors have begun embracing fresh approaches. Philanthropists have demanded and supported many new ventures in school operation, governance, financing, student recruitment, teacher training, and community partnership. Entirely new networks of Catholic schools have been created by social entrepreneurs and donors.

Parish schools have been nudged into sharing expertise and resources. Authority has been transferred in places to lay boards with much more management expertise than priests or bishops. Some schools have reorganized into networks independent of their parish or diocese while remaining fully Catholic. New programs at Catholic universities are

> How you behave, even more than what you know, is the greatest predictor of your long-term success. Catholic schools have known that for decades.

training more teachers and school leaders. Educators are using technology to modernize instruction and ease budget pressures. Some schools have specialized in areas like dual-language learning, classical models, or modern vocational education.

At the same time, public policies have grown much friendlier—driven mostly by philanthropic advocacy to school choice and parental options in education. Wisconsin broke ground with its 1989 voucher program, followed by other school-choice supports in Ohio in 1995, Arizona in 1997, Florida in 1999, and Pennsylvania in 2001. In the landmark 2002 case *Zelman v. Simmons-Harris,* the U.S. Supreme Court recognized scholarship programs that include religious schools to be Constitutional. There are now 57 (and growing) school-choice programs, managed by two-dozen states, that help nearly half a million students attend religious or private schools.

All of these changes leave Catholic schools better primed for a come-back than at any moment in the last half century. And these schools increasingly attract support from non-Catholic but public-spirited donors who did not previously give to this cause.

Why do we need Catholic schools anyway?

Catholic schools, like other non-governmental schools, retain a great deal of operational flexibility that district-run schools, and to a lesser extent charter schools, lack. Catholic schools are free of constraints related to educator certification, union rules, content standards, time requirements, and much more.

Catholic schools are also able to include religion and moral instruction within their activities. Faith and character development has been at the heart of Catholic schooling since its beginning, and remains an essential complement to academic development. "It's not what you know, but how you behave that's the greater predictor of your long-term success," notes Catholic-school donor Leo Linbeck III. "Catholic schools have known that and followed through with it for decades."

Catholic education also has a long history of superior academic outcomes, especially for historically underserved populations. In a summary of the research on the "Catholic school advantage," the Alliance for Catholic Education at the University of Notre Dame identifies the following results:

- Students in Catholic schools demonstrate higher academic achievement than similar students in district-run schools.
- The achievement gap between races and income groups is smaller in faith-based schools.
- Black and Latino students who attend Catholic schools are more likely to graduate from both high school and college than their peers from public schools.
- "Multiply disadvantaged" children particularly benefit from Catholic schools.
- Graduates of Catholic high schools earn higher wages than peers who graduate from public schools.
- Graduates of Catholic high schools are more likely to vote than their peers who graduate from public schools.
- Catholic school graduates are more civically engaged, more committed to service, and more tolerant of others.

Most Catholic schools produce academic results that are notably better than conventional public schools serving the same children. Their clearest successes lay outside of academics, however, in encouraging constructive, pro-social behavior. Few inner-city Catholic schools are at the same academic standard of today's very best charter schools. So there is lots of room for them to raise intellectual standards.

Donors impressed by the ways that Catholic schools already strengthen our society, and their potential to become even more successful, have countless opportunities to support and extend their good work. They can also speed improvement by trimming back in places where hidebound practices are *not* being updated.

"Sometimes withholding philanthropy is the best kind of assistance," argues Joe Womac of the Specialty Family Foundation. Christine Healey of the Healey Education Foundation suggests that "it's important to know when to say no—and be willing to follow through."

In this era of reinvention, Catholic-school donors also need to be tolerant of some risk. Investments in unproven approaches will be necessary if this large and valuable but still fragile social sector is to be updated. Risk is something that philanthropy is generally better positioned to handle than government or business.

"Failure is fine so long as it's not too expensive," says Dan Peters of the Ruth and Lovett Peters Foundation. "It's not a great hazard for a foundation or wealthy individual to spend $10,000 or $50,000 to try something new. We need to test things on a small scale. If it works, then expand it. If not, learn from it."

That sentiment was echoed by Stephanie Saroki de García, co-founder of Seton Education Partners. "Be willing to take risks—especially when you have a strong leader with a compelling idea," she advises. "Seton was founded in 2009, during the height of the recession, and we now provide nearly 2,200 high-quality, urban Catholic school seats. Startup funding is the hardest to find, but it reaps the greatest returns. We would not exist were it not for a handful of funders who took a chance on our leadership and ideas for a new way forward."

Some donors like to support innovation. Others fund only proven models. Many do something in between. Regardless of what category you fall in, we suggest there are three broad categories of activity where there are rich opportunities for you to support Catholic schools.

Certain donors will be most interested in direct financial help for students so they can access Catholic schools. Scholarships and similar initiatives can help families find, understand, and afford religious schooling. Chapter 2 provides ideas and strategies for such philanthropists.

Other donors may want to help individual schools or groups of schools improve and expand their operations and programming. There are many opportunities here: Replicating successful campuses. Helping the sector secure top teachers, principals, and business managers. Supporting new governance arrangements. Launching shared central-office capabilities. See Chapters 3 and 4 for information along these lines.

And there will also be donors who want to encourage systemic change. This can include advocating for improved public policies, or funding citywide reform agendas. Chapters 5 and 6 will delve into those approaches.

Whatever path today's donor chooses, he or she will find more opportunities for high returns on comparatively modest investments than most other social sectors can offer.

Helping Students Access Catholic Schools

The most direct way for donors to ensure that more students can enjoy the advantages of a Catholic-school education is to lift financial burdens that block students from attending. Scholarships are a tried-and-true way of immediately aiding students and families. A survey of key Catholic-school donors conducted by The Philanthropy Roundtable showed that more than a third of all grant dollars going to Catholic schools at present are channeled into student scholarships.

Finances are not the sole obstacle, though. Sometimes a simple lack of information that scholarships are available prevents families from even considering Catholic schools. More generally, a lack of knowledge about Catholic schools, their requirements, and their wide availability can be enrollment barriers. The effort of applying, and the need for advance planning before a school year begins, excludes some children. In places, non-English speakers are in the dark about Catholic schools. Relatively simple interventions from donors can address these kinds of access issues and information gaps that can prevent families from appreciating that they have educational choices.

In some places, simple but concentrated interventions will make it possible for hundreds of the families who most need and want Catholic schools to take action. For instance, the Latino community in some cities is ripe with opportunities for donors. The sheer number of Hispanic children in poverty today—5.7 million—is larger than the number of poor African-American or white children; many of these are struggling in inferior public schools. Yet only 300,000 Hispanic children currently attend Catholic schools. A recent report of Notre Dame's Alliance for Catholic Education set a short-term goal of increasing the percentage of Hispanic children to 6 percent (from today's 3 percent). This is an area where savvy donors could have powerful effects, working with an ethnic group that will constitute close to a third of all Americans by 2050.

Providing scholarships
A 2014 Georgetown University report found that 53 percent of Catholic parents identify tuition costs as "somewhat" or "very much" a problem when deciding whether or not to enroll their children in Catholic schools. Half of the parents who ultimately enroll their children say the same thing. Eliminating this barrier is the most direct way to help low-income students access a Catholic-school education.

"Scholarships are the simplest and most immediate way to help the most children across the board," states Rachel Elginsmith of the BASIC Fund, a Bay Area scholarship donor. "Getting kids into good schools is of the utmost urgency and too many kids are falling through the cracks every year. We need to get children into these schools, and scholarships do that."

The BASIC Fund provides partial-tuition scholarships so low-income K-8 students living in nine northern California counties can attend religious or private schools instead of a weak public school. Since its founding in 1998 the fund has supported 19,000 students at 300 local schools, half of them Catholic. In 2015 alone the BASIC Fund gave scholarships to more than 4,000 students, and the proportion using their award to attend a Catholic school had risen to three quarters.

A recent independent study of the fund's programs concluded that the academic performance of its recipient students improves after just one year. And although the BASIC Fund serves only children in grades K–8, these scholarships apparently prepare them for success in the years beyond: Sixty-five percent of BASIC Fund alumni subsequently win scholarships to religious or private high schools, and the high-school graduation rate of BASIC beneficiaries is over 95 percent.

Families must qualify financially for a BASIC stipend, then they are awarded on a first-come, first-served basis. Students must re-qualify financially every year, but once a student receives a scholarship, BASIC budgets to make sure funds will be available through the eighth grade. The cost to support an average student through his or her elementary schooling is $6,000.

Major gifts by individual donors and foundations supply the cash, though the fund has recently launched an innovative new Manzanita Fund that crowdsources fundraising for tuition scholarships. Community members, alumni, and current families are asked to give small amounts if they are able, to extend the fund's reach. Every $6,000 raised this way provides a scholarship to another child.

On the other side of the country, the Children's Scholarship Fund also provides grants to low-income children so they can attend Catholic schools. Since 1998, the New York City-based CSF has provided $168 million to 26,000 children living in its home metropolis. Currently, 8,300 children are attending 211 private elementary schools with the support of a CSF scholarship. A recent study showed that 92 percent of students receiving a CSF scholarship graduate from high school on time, and 90 percent enroll in college.

CSF has established partnerships and spurred spinoffs across the country. These include CSF–New Orleans, CSF–Baltimore, CSF–Portland, the Northwest Ohio Scholarship Fund, and others. The BASIC Fund is also a partner. Including all partner cities, the Children's Scholarship Fund has given 145,000 needy youngsters $610 million of scholarship gifts over a 16-year period.

Denver-based ACE Scholarships is one of CSF's local affiliates. Since 2000, it has provided 15,000 K–12 scholarships worth more than $25 million to children in its city. These scholarships work: In 2011, 91 percent of ACE students graduated from high school. In 2010, ACE's low-income students had an average ACT score of 20.3—far above the 16.1 and 16.0 averages for low-income students in Colorado and Denver respectively.

Not every state has a CSF-affiliated scholarship program, but similar programs exist in many areas, allowing donors opportunities to support poor children in Catholic and other private schools. For example, Cincinnati's Catholic Inner-city Schools Education Fund provides financial support to eight elementary schools serving approximately 1,800 students in low-income neighborhoods. Because Ohio offers state-funded vouchers, two thirds of students attending CISE schools receive state help, but the Catholic schools' operating costs are substantially higher than the voucher amount. CISE helps fill that gap with grants that cover approximately a quarter of school costs.

Cincinnati's Catholic schools are again of a demonstrably high quality. All of CISE third-grade students are reading at grade level—an important milestone that far outpaces the national average for low-income children. In 2013, just 20 percent of low-income fourth graders tested proficient or higher on the NAEP reading assessment. Results outside the classroom in behavior, health, and happiness are also apparent. With accomplishments like these, CISE has been able to raise tens of millions of dollars from donors to improve Cincinnati's Catholic schools.

In addition to its elementary-school program, CISE runs a donor-directed grant program that provides tuition assistance to students who want to attend local Catholic high schools. Backers like the Farmer Family Foundation, the Lester Besl Family Foundation, the Evelyn and Charles Burgoyne Foundation, and individual donors like Donald and Catharine Laden expanded this grant program from $75,000 in 2001 to more than $800,000 in 2013.

In September 2015, the Inner-city Scholarship Fund run by the Archdiocese of New York City announced the largest-ever U.S. gift to Catholic schooling. Christine and Stephen Schwarzman gave a record $40 million to create an endowment that will provide 2,900 children per year with scholarships. Since the Schwarzmans started contributing to scholarships in 2001, "we've met so many impressive young women and men," said Christine, "who have benefited greatly from the values provided by a Catholic-school education." The Inner-city Scholarship Fund combines contributions from New York business leaders and church donors, and provided tuition assistance to nearly 7,000 Catholic-school students in 2015, prior to the Schwarzman gift.

Direct school support, plus wider efforts

Some scholarship organizations go beyond simply providing tuition aid to students, and provide direct support to the schools themselves. The Big Shoulders Fund does this in inner-city Chicago. Over the last 25 years it has raised more than $215 million for inner-city Catholic education in that city.

The Big Shoulders Fund pays for special-education programs, buys instructional equipment, improves facilities, supports faculty, and provides operating grants to Catholic schools that serve the neediest neighborhoods of Chicago. (It also makes student-scholarship grants.) Currently, schools benefiting from the Big Shoulders Fund enroll nearly 25,000 students in 76 elementary schools and 17 high schools across Chicago, the oldest and poorest such institutions in the archdiocese. Seventy-nine percent of the beneficiary students are minority, and 62 percent live in poverty. Despite these obstacles, 87 percent of the high-school seniors graduate and continue into college education.

The Fulcrum Foundation in Seattle is another donor consortium that has helped many needy students access Catholic schools since its founding in 2002. Approximately 60 percent of Fulcrum's annual giving takes the form of tuition assistance. "We provide $1,200 scholarships that are making a tremendous impact," explains executive director Anthony Holter. "Now we're working to grow our funds to move up the income ladder and into middle-class tuition assistance."

Fulcrum doesn't just fuel the existing schools, though; it works hard to make them better. The foundation has created an incentive program that requires participating schools to adopt practices likely to improve student-learning levels. "We've moved from only grantmaking to investing in human-capital development and insisting on best business practices and management. We realized we needed to invest more resources into excellence." Fulcrum now pays for things like improved management, better marketing, and an Office of Catholic Schools headquarters.

Other philanthropists have begun thinking differently about providing scholarships to students. Donor John Hazeltine has suggested imitating Kiva.org, a nonprofit that fights developing-world poverty by linking millions of small donors to millions of small borrowers. Kiva provides potential recipients a place to tell their stories and ask for loans to grow businesses, go to school, buy clean cooking fuel, and more. Donors who read these stories can make a loan to the borrower of their choice. On-the-ground "field partners" (local organizations within the communities where the loans are being used) vet borrowers, disburse the loans, and provide updates to lenders as the borrowers expend and eventually repay their loans.

Hazeltine's idea is to apply the human-interest aspects and efficient bundling mechanisms of Kiva and other crowdfunding platforms to Catholic-school scholarships. Involving lots of small givers could yield sharp increases in scholarship funding. The concept hit Hazeltine out of personal experience: "We gave our first multiyear tuition assistance pledge to benefit a K-8 student who lost his dad to a heart attack. The student was attending the same school as our children, and we knew the boy, his potential, and the circumstances of

> Donors who provide scholarships to students can strongly influence individual lives. That has been demonstrated many times, to the thrill of givers.

his family. We remained anonymous. Later a pastor asked us privately to provide tuition aid to other identified individuals based on their specific narratives."

There are aspects of this that would need to be solved before it could be launched. For instance, can compelling narratives be produced without revealing personal information about students in undesired ways? But tech-enabled matching systems like Uber, Airbnb, and numerous crowdfunding websites have shown that problems like these can be solved, involving wide circles of population in cooperative efforts, once kinks are worked out. There is no question about whether donors who provide scholarships to students can strongly influence individual lives. That has been demonstrated many times, to the thrill of givers. Crowdfunding might fit perfectly with Catholic-school scholarships, bringing satisfactions to thousands of small donors.

Another "different" approach through which philanthropists can help bring Catholic education to families hungry for better options is through structural change. Darla Romfo, director of the Children's Scholarship Fund, suggests this should include work like "educating interest groups about the broader importance of parental choice. It involves building and protecting tax credits, vouchers, and other vehicles in each state. It requires protecting nonprofit schools that don't receive taxpayer support, which will stay alive and flourish in the marketplace of education only with the long-term support of committed philanthropists."

"As I look at all of the places where parental choice has expanded since CSF was founded in 1998, at least ten of the additional programs were championed by CSF supporters. We will never overestimate the power of helping one child reach his or her full potential through a scholarship. But we must also work for the day when every child will have truly good educational options." (Chapter 5 is all about ways donors can push for a friendlier environment for school choice.)

These goals often overlap and reinforce each other. For instance, funding scholarships can help schools stabilize enrollment, thus preserving a school or even a whole group of schools. That allows managers to redirect attention to bigger subjects like governance, operational efficiency, curriculum, and transparency. Then supporters can put new emphasis on marketing, advocating for fairer public policies, and other big-picture work. At that point, creating new schools, or expanding existing schools, becomes practical.

"Scholarships offer great satisfaction," notes leading Catholic-schools donor and venture capitalist B. J. Cassin. "But if you're able to invest a dollar in the startup of a new school, and have other foundations add more, you've amplified your investments." Thus scholarships can be both an immediate boon to families, and philanthropists' gateway into making wider waves.

Getting children off of waiting lists

Another way donors can support students in accessing Catholic schools is by letting parents know such schools are an option. The best charter schools have large and growing waiting lists of students who would like to attend—over a thousand individuals at some schools. More than a million students were waiting in a queue in 2013 to get into a charter school that lacked room for them. Yet desks sometimes sit empty in nearby high-quality Catholic schools. Some parents feel they cannot afford the Catholic alternative (which, as we have seen, is often untrue thanks to scholarships, though this is not adequately appreciated). Other parents, however, are simply unaware that Catholic schools are an option for their families. Donors have a huge opportunity to bridge this gap.

Organizations like Families Empowered in Houston help families on charter-school waitlists learn about and access other high-quality school options, including Catholic schools. Families Empowered provides information about schools in various neighborhoods, details of enrollment, and more. The organization uses phone calls, e-mail, social media, and choice fairs to communicate with families about their other charter, district, magnet, Catholic, and independent school options.

When families apply to either KIPP or YES Prep charter schools in Houston—both of which are high quality but heavily over-subscribed networks—they can check a box to have their information shared with Families Empowered. If the family ends up on a KIPP or YES Prep waitlist, Families Empowered contacts them and provides information about other available options. Parents can also contact Families Empowered directly if they are seeking information about additional school options.

Families Empowered has worked with the Houston Catholic Archdiocese from the beginning, publicizing local Catholic schools and scholarship opportunities. "This is a win–win for everyone," explains FE director Colleen Dippel. "Charters can't serve all the kids on their waitlists, but they still want them to be successful. We're committed to supporting Catholic schools because we need them to be a viable option for parents. There's huge potential to close the gap if all the waitlisted kids get into other good schools. Making Catholic schools a viable option for families further accelerates the flywheel of choice."

In a system of choice, easily accessible information is crucial. Yet there is often less about local Catholic-school performance in public circulation than would be desirable.

This year, Families Empowered piloted an "open-seat campaign." School leaders identify the number of open seats in their schools, and Families Empowered reaches out to families in their database, simultaneously sending schools a spreadsheet containing contact information for prospective students. The schools follow up with these families directly.

Families Empowered plans to expand this effort to include additional Catholic schools next year. A local donor has funded this work, allowing Families Empowered to play matchmaker between families in need and Catholic schools. The schools that receive these lists of interested families are required to have the infrastructure to manage increased inquiries and enrollments. This means designating staff to answer phones, respond to questions, get back to parents, walk families through the application process, take them on campus tours, and ultimately serve them as enrolled customers.

Many Catholic schools are weak when it comes to advertising and explaining themselves. In a system of choice, easily accessible information is crucial, yet there is often less easy public circulation on the programs, performance, and staffing of Catholic schools than would be desirable. Overworked principals, uneasiness with marketing, timidity, or simple inertia can reduce the transparency of Catholic schools. Fixing this can be a valuable new avenue for donors.

In most states, Catholic schools don't administer the same student-achievement assessments as public schools, making comparisons a challenge. Catholic schools should at least develop their own easily tracked measures of school performance. Donors could encourage and help Catholic educators to establish consistent industry standards like a common school-performance report card. This should include a full range of important outcome indicators: achievement levels, graduation rates, AP participation, and so forth, as well as parent, teacher, and student satisfaction surveys, measures of school culture and mission effectiveness, cost data, extracurricular participation rates, elements related to Catholic identity, such as Mass attendance and volunteer hours, and evidence on student character and leadership.

Philanthropists could make adherence to these standards a condition of grants. Industry standards in other areas might also make sense. Colleen Dippel of Families Empowered notes that the Archdiocese of Galveston lacks a centralized enrollment system for all of its schools. This means that the superintendent has no way of knowing or projecting school population patterns, or of targeting outreach for specific schools or grade levels. Internal planning and resource allocation is consequently challenging. Donors could help Catholic schools standardize management and business systems, and invest in new technology or software that makes crucial information easy to use in personnel, marketing, and resource-allocation decisions.

Once again we are reminded: For a system of choice to work well, it needs more than just scholarships. Do families know what schools are available? Which have open seats? Is there information available on each school's mission and performance? Is it easy for families to apply to schools? Do school networks have systems for managing vital

Los Angeles donors pay for openness

Joe Womac of the Specialty Family Foundation and Sister Rosemarie Nassif of the Conrad Hilton Foundation invited Los Angeles donors to come together for an open conversation about successes and challenges in working with Catholic schools. Representatives from 25 area philanthropies showed up. By the close of the meeting, participants had identified two top issues they thought they could better solve together than alone: data transparency and governance.

Choosing to focus on data transparency first—a potentially less controversial topic than governance—the leaders of the collaborative approached school leaders and the Office of Catholic Schools to develop a shared definition of "transparency." One of the biggest lessons here, explains Sister Rosemarie, was "realizing that 'transparency' meant different things to each of us.... The 'aha' moment came when we defined it the same way."

Once a common definition of the things that every school should make public had been crafted, the donors' collaborative hired an outside consultant to work with the Office of Catholic Schools to create an academic report card or "snapshot" of each Catholic school's progress. The snapshot covers performance in three areas: faith, academics, and stewardship. Each area has a set of measurable indicators. For example, the faith category lists the percent of teachers who are certified in Christian instruction. Academic assessment includes student progress on standardized assessments administered throughout the year.

Funders in the collaborative funded the development of these report cards. Schools in turn agreed to provide all necessary information. All parties agreed this format provides much-needed understanding and openness, though at present the findings are only used narrowly—one of the compromises made during negotiations is that this report-card data is solely for schools and funders. School leaders may choose to share it with parents or other stakeholders, but there is no requirement that they do so.

Down the road, that extra level of information sharing should be encouraged by donors.

One of the major improvements in public schooling over the past two decades has been the publication of comparable student-achievement data and other important information on the functioning of individual schools. These report cards have enlightened parents and policymakers and helped spur much needed change. Report-card systems for Catholic schools could prove similarly useful in encouraging excellence and accountability.

Creation of the Los Angeles report card cost less than $100,000 in total, a remarkably small investment for a treasure-trove of information. Donors had been frustrated for years by the lack of data, and many had tried individually to get pieces of the puzzle. But it wasn't until they made their request in combination that they were able to coalesce around a clear goal and convince the schools to develop a solution. The Los Angeles Donors Collaborative is a terrific example of the power of philanthropists to bring about important change at a modest cost. With the right leadership, this kind of joint effort should take place in many other cities, and be expanded to shine even greater light, for an even wider circle of interested parties, on educational results, needs, and trends over time.

information? Donors will be crucial in all of these areas, and can have very large effects if they will become involved.

Building citywide common enrollment systems

In cities like Houston, where school enrollment is decentralized and individual schools have different application processes and deadlines, organizations like Families Empowered are valuable resources for families. In other places, school enrollment has been standardized through a shared system that allows families to apply to a range of schools through one portal. The most advanced public-school systems include a common submission date across all participating schools: one form that allows families to apply to all of their preferred schools and rank their choices, a common algorithm that matches students with schools, and an appeals process for families dissatisfied with their school assignment.

Unfortunately these unified platforms are still the exception, and those that exist usually meld only conventional public schools and charter schools. Leadership and funding from the Bill & Melinda Gates Foundation has recently pulled several cities with lots of charters into "Collaboration Compacts." These include efforts to standardize school calendars and ultimately unify enrollment mechanisms so parents can place children in charters and district-run schools from one place. In Philadelphia and Boston the Gates Compacts have even folded the archdiocese Catholic schools into the collaboration, making it a three-sector effort, with discussion of common enrollment calendars being one of the topics.

The OneApp system in New Orleans, bankrolled in part by the Walton Family Foundation, includes private and religious schools. The state of Louisiana operates a private-school voucher program through which students can receive scholarships to attend Catholic schools and private schools. Families in New Orleans can use OneApp to choose from traditional district, charter, religious, or private schools all in the same application.

This common enrollment system is part of a larger effort to make the New Orleans schools neutral about what type of learning environment parents select. Michael Stone of New Schools for New Orleans reports that "Right now, our unified enrollment system includes almost every public school in the city, as well as our private and parochial scholarship schools. Next year, the enrollment program will expand to include any pre-K program in the city that uses public funds—public, private, or religious. We're moving toward a 'one-sector' approach in other ways as well. The Urban League of Greater New Orleans, for instance, publishes a high-school guide that provides information on public, private, and parochial high schools across New Orleans."

Adam Hawf, former assistant superintendent at the Louisiana Department of Education, explains that the inclusion of religious and private schools in OneApp "gave them shelf space in a mainstream system, and allowed parents to access the full range of options in a format that allows for true comparability across schools. It's been really good for schools and for families."

Currently 29 states and the District of Columbia have some type of private-school choice program in place (those programs are discussed later in this book). Very few of these have a common enrollment system that includes Catholic and other private schools, however. A common enrollment system could ease burdens on families, and serve as a "market-enabler" that helps make parental exercise of school choice real rather than just a theoretical option. It would clarify the performance of different schools, allow easy comparisons, and force all schools to compete for students. Paying for creation of a common enrollment system in your city could thus be a very strategic philanthropic investment.

Welcoming Hispanics into Catholic schools

More than a decade ago when the American Catholic bishops wrote *Renewing Our Commitment*, they vowed to "serve the increasing Hispanic/ Latino population…. Catholic parishes and schools must reflect this reality and reach out to welcome Hispanics." The U.S. Hispanic population rose to 55 million in 2015, six times the level of 1970. While its growth rate has recently slowed, the U.S. Census Bureau projects that the Hispanic population may reach 129 million by 2060.

Hispanics make up 40 percent of all U.S. Catholics, yet only 3 percent of school-aged Latino children are enrolled in Catholic schools.

Hispanics are already the largest minority group in the United States. Fully one quarter of U.S. elementary-age children are Hispanic today; in some southern and western states the figure is close to half. Over the next generation the fraction nationwide will rise to one third.

Among Latino adults, 55 percent identify themselves as Catholic. Hispanics make up approximately 40 percent of all U.S. Catholics, and a much higher percentage of parent-age Catholics. Yet only 3 percent of school-aged Latino children are enrolled in Catholic schools.

There are a variety of explanations for this. Many Hispanic immigrants had no tradition of Catholic schools in their home countries. Affordability is a barrier, both for families and for churches sponsoring schools. A 2009 report by the Alliance for Catholic Education found that cost was the number one issue for Hispanic families that did not send their children to Catholic school. A Boston College study found that parishes where 75 percent or more of mass attendees are Hispanic collect less than half the revenue of parishes where 75 percent or more are non-Hispanic.

However, ACE research suggests that income accounts for only about one third of the discrepancy between Hispanic and non-Hispanic use of Catholic schools. Culture gaps keep many Hispanic families from seeking out parochial schools—Spanish language is a particular barrier. Though "our schools for years and years served immigrants," says the Reverend Joe Corpora of ACE, "we've never reinvented them to serve *today's* immigrants."

"Everyone—bishops, superintendents, pastors, principals, school boards, parents—is interested in this initiative of enrolling more Latino children in our Catholic schools," says Corpora. "The entire approach to recruiting and welcoming Hispanic families and children is different from how one would recruit non-Hispanic children."

Corpora has developed a list of 20 simple things Catholic leaders can do to help make their schools more hospitable to Latino families. These include learning basic Spanish phrases, advertising in Spanish, spotlighting culturally relevant religious imagery (e.g. Our Lady of Guadalupe), teaching the Mass in Spanish, including Latino families on school advisory councils, inviting Spanish-speaking priests to visit the school, even putting a "Bienvenidos" (Welcome) sign by the front door. He recommends that donors interested in being helpful fund a "field consultant" for schools, or an entire diocese. "Thirteen dioceses have done this, and all are increasing enrollment. The costs of hiring someone are quickly recovered if even a handful of new students enrolled."

In addition to generating less income, there are data indicating that heavily Hispanic parishes are less likely to take responsibility for a local Catholic school. Only 34 percent of parishes where half or more of members are Hispanic take responsibility for a school, compared to 60 percent of parishes where less than a quarter of the population is Hispanic. Some of the dioceses with the lowest ratio of Catholic-school students are cities with heavy Hispanic populations—like Brownsville, Fresno, El Paso, San Bernardino, Laredo, Pueblo, Fort Worth, and Dallas.

In 2008, Notre Dame president John Jenkins commissioned a task force to investigate ways of increasing the access of Hispanic families to Catholic schools. The task force analyzed four major areas: school environment, marketing, finance, and school leadership. Its 2009 report, *To Nurture the Soul of a Nation*, recommends very practical steps: asking priests in heavily Hispanic parishes to emphasize Catholic education, encouraging families to seek more information on Catholic schools, and having schools identify Spanish-speaking liaisons to support the families who do reach out.

Informed by these findings, the Alliance for Catholic Education launched a "Catholic-school advantage campaign" designed to both promote the value of Catholic schools within the Latino community and to help existing Catholic schools respond to the needs of Latino families. In 2014, Bishop Daniel Flores of Brownsville, Texas, urged his fellow bishops to actively recruit Hispanic families into schools. "If efforts are not made to reach out to them, they won't think it's a viable option," he explained.

Donors can support this process in a number of ways.

- *Support Spanish language outreach* Donors can pay for targeted marketing, help school leaders translate documents into Spanish, make sure that volunteers are available to support families in understanding and accessing schools, and pay for Spanish-speaking staff.
- *Fund cultural training and bilingual curricula* More broadly, professional development for teachers and addition of bilingual instructional capacity may be needed.
- *Adjust funding mechanisms* If Hispanic families are to be attracted, schools need help in maximizing tuition subsidies without bankrupting the institution. This may require increased scholarships, creation of endowments, better planning for multiyear tuition subsidies, and for extending scholarships to siblings of enrolled children.
- *Create more schools* If parishes serving Latino families don't operate Catholic schools, marketing is useless. Donors should consider working with dioceses, pastors, and religious orders to start new schools where they are needed. (Chapter 3 focuses on new school models.)
- *Provide leaders with resources* Principals and superintendents at notoriously lean Catholic schools will need extra time, staff assistance, and money if they are to add aggressive student recruitment and family outreach to existing responsibilities.
- *Advocate for school choice* Donors can press political leaders to start or expand school-choice programs offering publicly funded scholarships, vouchers, tax credits, or savings accounts, particularly in states with large Hispanic populations. Where such options already exist, donors can help Hispanic families enter and navigate these programs. (Advocacy is discussed more generally in Chapter 5.)
- *Underwrite a part-time liaison* ACE recommends starting a "Madrinas Program." Madrinas are trusted Latina women who have their children in Catholic schools; they serve as a point of contact and a source of help for Hispanic families. Madrinas can serve as translators, help fill out applications, and keep families informed about

school issues. According to Father Corpora, a Madrina can be a low-dollar, high-impact investment: "Donors could help fund a Madrina, which in many cases is just a stipend of $500 or so."

Efforts have been launched in recent years to help donors fund measures like those listed above. Three broad initiatives illustrate some of the possibilities. The first is the Hispanic Recruitment Initiative begun in 2008 by the Catholic Schools Foundation of Boston. Made possible through a gift by the Birmingham Foundation, the HRI helps area schools identify barriers to increasing Latino enrollment and then address them.

The School Pastors' Institute was started in 2011 to train pastors of Catholic schools across the country. It offers four-day conferences on the campus of the University of Notre Dame with workshops on topics like Catholic culture and identity, and financial management and advancement. And it has made topics like welcoming of Latino children and families part of its basic curriculum. Since its start, more than 380 pastors have participated.

The Latino Enrollment Institute, created in 2012, assists Catholic schools with open seats and substantial numbers of Latino families in the surrounding area in attracting Hispanic students. Principals and select faculty leaders get trained in four-day summer programs on Notre Dame's campus. Leaders from 80 schools participated in the organization's first couple of years, resulting in documented increases in Hispanic enrollment at nearly all of them.

Investing in Promising New Models

There is a considerable consensus today that the traditional Catholic school run by the local church is unsustainable in many places. "Putting all power with the pastor is great when the pastor is amazing and has the desire and capacity to be intricately involved in the day-to-day operations of the school," says Joe Womac of the Specialty Family Foundation in Los Angeles. "Unfortunately, this parish model no longer reflects reality, with many pastors being stretched too thin and lacking the capacity to be meaningfully involved in running a school." What's needed, he says, are new governance models. Investor and donor Tony de Nicola agrees that without changes in the way schools are managed "we'll continue to face the same challenges."

When The Philanthropy Roundtable asked Catholic-school donors about barriers to the sector's growth, 69 percent named "diocesan bureaucracy." The experience of the GHR Foundation of Minnesota will be familiar to many donors. "The GHR Foundation had been funding Catholic schools for a number of years and putting in a lot of money," explains Meg Gehlen Nodzon. This included a $1 million grant to the local diocese for scholarships and other purposes. Nevertheless, "schools were still financially unstable and ran the gamut, academically, from highly effective to questionable."

Changing times require a new approach to organizing Catholic education, argues John Eriksen, former superintendent of schools for the diocese of Paterson, New Jersey. "Dioceses feel that in order to control their schools they need to manage all schools. That's a mistake. I would much rather see dioceses bid out the management of these schools to other operators."

At its core, governance is about who has power. The ultimate authority over a Catholic school usually resides with the local bishop. His degree of involvement, however, ranges widely.

Bishops are allowed to delegate responsibilities of running schools, and often do. Many regions have a secretary of education, vicar general, or superintendent of local Catholic schools. The commonest arrangement has been for priests to delegate operational responsibilities to school principals. The only responsibilities that cannot be delegated relate to the religious and moral teachings of the school.

Changing the way Catholic schools are organized, operated, and governed means overturning more than a century's worth of practice. "There are certain things you have to break to fix the system: old mindsets, old staffing models, old ways of governing schools, old ways of being held accountable," says Casey Carter of Philadelphia's Faith in the Future. The next generation of healthy schools "is going to look very different from schools and approaches of the past."

Understandably, many priests and bishops are hesitant about altering longstanding customs and formulas. But resistance seems to be softening. Unprecedented new arrangements for governing the Catholic schools that have been put into place in prominent locations like New York City and Philadelphia are speeding the pace of change.

Since 2009, Notre Dame's Alliance for Catholic Education has hosted a series of meetings among bishops to discuss the revitalization of Catholic K-12 schooling. The resulting conversations have helped open minds about system updates. ACE's John Schoenig sees "growing receptivity among bishops to new models. The paradigm has shifted fundamentally in these six years."

> Changing the way Catholic schools are governed means overturning more than a century's worth of practice.

The question is no longer whether Catholic schools should be run differently; it's about how. "There's strong understanding about the concept of alternative governance," says Schoenig. "Now the bishops are considering details and degree. There are different ways we can do this, different approaches to authority, different organizational structures. We're discussing all of the possibilities."

The explorations have extended far beyond talk—new approaches are now being tested, honed, and expanded from coast to coast. And bishops aren't the only ones in these conversations. Donors, school administrators, teachers, lay leaders, and many others are involved. By insisting on updated structures and helping to pay for them, donors can have a powerful influence on this crucial transition.

Fostering change within traditional governance structures

"I want to work within the system as an agent for positive change collaborating with the bishops and their staffs," says philanthropist Tony de Nicola. "This is what I do with companies I own through private equity. I work with CEOs to make them better."

Donors who are in that camp may want to encourage school administrators to share information and resources in loose consortia. This step appeals to some because it is less disruptive than the governing change we'll consider in the next section. Yet it still offers chances to improve management and sustainability by getting schools to cooperate.

Consortia vary. Some support a small number of schools in a small geographic space—like the Consortium of Catholic Academies, a nonprofit created to provide administrative, curricular, and financial support to four schools in Washington, D.C., that collectively educate about 800 students every year. It dates to 2007 when plans were announced to convert seven of D.C.'s 14 Catholic schools into charter schools (see the "Catholic-school conversions" section later in this chapter for more on this topic). Four of the remaining schools were reorganized under the CCA umbrella.

Other consortia link schools across geographic boundaries. For example, the Mid-Atlantic Catholic Schools Consortium shares seven activities—including procurement, leadership development, and joint advocacy—among members stretching from D.C. to Baltimore to Wilmington, Delaware. The Greater Milwaukee Catholic Education Consortium was formed in 2007 by the deans of the five Catholic universities in Milwaukee and supported by a startup donation from the Stollenwerk Family Foundation. Its mission is to support and revitalize the Catholic schools in that city by marshaling academic resources and expertise from the adjoining Catholic colleges.

Donor John Stollenwerk, former owner of Allen Edmonds Shoes, explains the program's genesis: "Cardinal Dolan [then Archbishop of Milwaukee] and I came up with idea of putting the five Catholic colleges and their incredible resources to use for the benefit of Catholic schools. Each college puts some money into it, according to size, and then they charge a small fee for the program. It wasn't hard to get the colleges involved. They saw the need, and also an opportunity to work with teachers pursuing post-graduate degree programs."

The Milwaukee consortium behaves much like a consulting firm. It helps develop teacher and principal skills, bolsters fundraising, marketing, and public relations, and strengthens management. It also provides schools with expertise and resources when new needs pop up—like vocational skills training, or anti-bullying instruction. The consortium holds large workshops, sponsors intimate conversations, and consults on site.

The work of the Catholic School Consortium in Los Angeles has been driven almost entirely by philanthropy. In 2008 the Specialty Family Foundation invited 13 schools to join together to strengthen their development, marketing, and outreach activities. Nine schools took up the offer. Each received a three-year grant of $250,000 to hire a staff member to lead development, and to meet monthly with his or her peers from the other schools to share ideas and challenges.

The consortium now unites two dozen schools, and the scope of their work has expanded. For example, nine of the member schools recently joined forces to hire an accounting firm to handle all of their books. Three schools partnered with a local university to align their teacher professional development. The goal of the program is to build the competence of schools to the point where no ongoing support from Specialty is needed, and where "a sustainable, vibrant, rigorous Catholic elementary school will be available to every Los Angeles area child who seeks to attend regardless of ability to pay."

The consortium, which spun itself into an independent 501(c)(3) in 2014, is making a difference for many of its participants. Two schools "are absolutely night and day different over a five-to-seven year period," reports Joe Womac of Specialty. "At least three additional campuses were good schools that have become great, maintaining both excellence and financial health. These schools prove it can be done in the inner-city."

Fostering change by transforming governance

A new generation of school networks—sometimes called "private-school management organizations"—has gained attention for leading groups of Catholic schools toward greater success. These organizations offer the benefits of the consortia just discussed—like knowledge trading and shared services—but go much further to create common operating practices built on shared leadership and mission. Unlike consortia, creating these managed networks of schools requires an all-new kind of governance and control.

Every network has a central office that standardizes budgeting, hiring, fundraising, procurement, curriculum, and building acquisition and management. This frees up principals to focus on instruction, and religious leaders to focus on spiritual and moral guidance. This arrangement has in several instances produced chains of schools that are financially sustainable and academically excellent.

The question is no longer whether Catholic schools should be run differently; it's about how.

To make this new structure work, a diocese must be willing to devolve most school governing authority to the private school management organization. Though still quite new, PSMOs are already diversifying into different types. In some cases a bishop grants operating

A Minneapolis center of excellence

A group of lay leaders, funders, principals, and pastors set out to create a new structure to manage the Catholic schools in Minneapolis-St. Paul. Their original idea was to create a new entity that would directly run 10 to 15 schools, and provide support and services to 90 Catholic schools in the Twin Cities. But a crisis intervened and this new organization never got off the ground.

Criminal behavior and financial improprieties by priests brought legal charges, resignations, and a bankruptcy disaster to the Minneapolis-St. Paul Archdiocese. Part of the fallout was the shuttering of the Office of Catholic Schools. Richard Schulze, founder of Best Buy and of the Richard M. Schulze Family Foundation, stepped in to help fill this breach.

The Schulze Family Foundation invited all of the region's Catholic school leaders to meet together. Those attending said they'd never met three quarters of the others in the room, according to Schulze's Steve Hoeppner, revealing serious gaps in communications and collaboration. Afterward, foundation staff visited all K-8 schools in the metro area and interviewed each

principal. "It wasn't about telling them what to do," said Hoeppner. "We want to help the schools academically, operationally, and spiritually, but we don't want to impose practices." These interviews revealed overarching problems of decreasing enrollment and increasing costs. They also spotlighted specific needs like better teacher training, improved technology, more marketing, support for high-need students, and modernized development and outreach plans.

Armed with these findings, Richard Schulze worked to identify other local donors willing to become partners in support of Catholic elementary schools. The GHR Foundation, the local Catholic Community Foundation, and the Aim Higher Foundation agreed to join forces, and the Catholic Schools Center of Excellence was born as an independent 501(c)(3). Gail Dorn, a former vice president at Target, was hired as president and the organization launched in 2015.

Early projects inaugurated by the center included a webinar to train principals on personal tech devices like iPads, and a workshop on managing student enrollment processes. More than 100 principals and school leaders signed up to attend these. As this is written the center is working with schools to develop a centralized purchasing process that will reduce costs.

"We're really just trying to get as much help out there as possible," says Hoeppner. "We want to be there for the schools as an approachable support system. We want schools to come to us for help." The center does not charge for its services.

There are many lessons for donors in this initiative. The comprehensive assessment of needs via principal interviews, the collaboration among multiple funders, the development of a new external organization to provide tailored support, and other aspects are eminently copyable. Donors interested in helping their local schools might start by asking three questions: Do we know what our schools need? Are external partners for meeting their needs available? Do we have, or can we form, an organization able to provide goods and services?

and management authority over a set of schools to a board that functions as the governing body. In other cases operating and management authority is granted to a foundation or other external entity. In all cases the new entity has limits on its jurisdiction, but it looks a lot like the headquarters of a charter-school chain that sets consistent standards across campuses.

These new management organizations have exciting potential to bring not only good performance but also sustained expansion to Catholic schooling—something the old Catholic-school structure has found almost impossible for generations. Where the goal is to bring high-quality Catholic schooling to new students, specially managed networks of schools are likely to be the most effective tool. If donors will strengthen and improve them, these networks have potential to become one of this era's major contributions to Catholic education, as demonstrated by the examples that follow.

Jubilee Schools

Between 1999 and 2004, donors helped the Diocese of Memphis reopen several closed Catholic schools. A massive philanthropic gift provided both operational funds and an endowment. The so-called "Jubilee" schools now serve more than 1,200 low-income students in Memphis' inner-city neighborhoods.

In 2010, former charter-school leader David Hill was named director of academic operations. He instituted changes across the network—extending the school day, strengthening school culture, putting more emphasis on attracting and retaining high-quality teachers and principals. This seems to be paying dividends in academic performance.

Financial challenges, however, continue. The schools serve the most impoverished families in the region, without public funds, and the housing-foreclosure recession forced the network to dip into its endowment. (Many donors have found endowments to be ephemeral solutions that don't last.) In October 2014, Bishop Terry Steib announced that the nine Jubilee Schools would spin off from the diocese as the Jubilee Catholic Schools Network, with Hill as president. It is intended that the network's new independence will make fundraising easier.

Hill is now in charge of all aspects of the schools, including academics, business, and fundraising. He reports to overseeing directors. "We now have a new board that governs these schools exclusively," he notes, and have "been given broad latitude and autonomy to make decisions." He intends to "increase the work of the network while reducing the operational demands on principals. We wanted to free them to focus more on being academic leaders."

The first major change since becoming an independent network has been a new school calendar, and correlated changes in teacher and principal compensation. Starting with the 2015-2016 school year, the Jubilee Schools will operate on a 200-day, year-round calendar.

Hill stresses that formation of the independent Jubilee Schools Network will in no way alter the schools' Catholic foundation: "There seems to be an underlying fear that this change means our schools are becoming charter schools. That is not the case. Our schools will not lose their Catholic identities through this transition. If anything it's going to strengthen our Catholicity," he told us in an interview.

Catholic Partnership Schools

In 2005 there were just five Catholic elementary schools left in inner-city Camden, New Jersey, and three of them were scheduled to close. But donor Christine Healey convinced the bishop to put off the closures and give her a chance to manage the vulnerable schools. The two other remaining elementary schools also signed on. The Healey Education Foundation and the diocese set up a board of limited jurisdiction that would acquire all decision-making power regarding the management of the schools, while leaving the bishop authority over the religious doctrine of the schools and a few other matters. The board incorporated its own 501(c)(3) in 2010 known as Catholic Partnership Schools.

After researching the dilemma, Healey explains, she determined that a conventional approach wouldn't work. The bolder network model was essential. "Before we started, I researched about 40 consortium models of Catholic schools across the country. Most were run within dioceses and they'd simply clustered schools that were struggling in urban settings. I analyzed those, and many weren't effective. Pulling a group of failing enterprises together for economies of scale in things like purchasing isn't enough. Most of these clusters continued to be managed within dioceses that don't have the skills and resources to make tough decisions and find and manage the right talent. Urban Catholic schools need different operating systems and structures to be successful."

Under the Camden governing arrangement, local priests are no longer responsible for many of the operational aspects of the school, including payroll, finances, facilities, fundraising, academics, and curriculum. Partnership director Sister Karen Dietrich meets with all five principals on a monthly basis to establish common high standards and consistent businesslike practices. One welcome result of the Partnership is the sense of community that the principals now feel. The Camden diocese sprawls, and the needs of its suburban school principals are quite different from those of the principals of its inner-city schools.

While unifying many practices, the Partnership has given each of the five schools latitude to maintain cultural distinctions. "The neighborhoods of these schools are unique, and most of the schools have been in place since the 1920s," explains Sister Dietrich. "They are anchors for their communities and significant to the neighborhood. We want to honor their history and ensure the schools maintain their community character."

The Partnership relies almost entirely on private support. Donors include the Healey foundation, regional philanthropies, and individuals. The national Children's Scholarship Fund has a strong long-time alliance with the Partnership, providing an annual matching grant that helps several hundred boys and girls attend one of its five schools.

Cristo Rey

In 2000, venture capitalist and Catholic-school champion B. J. Cassin created a foundation to help replicate successful schools. He provided $12 million to create a spinoff of the Cristo Rey Jesuit High School, a Chicago innovation with an unusual structure and impressive results. When its creators first opened the high school in 1996 to an overwhelmingly low-income Hispanic population, they faced the same vexing problem that haunts many Catholic schools: how to provide a high-quality education, without any public funds, to a low-income community that cannot afford to pay much tuition. Their solution was a corporate work-study program. At the original campus, and at each new spinoff, students are required to work five days each month in an entry-level job through the school's corporate work study program.

Four-student teams share a single full-time job. Each member works one full day per week in the position; every fourth week a team member puts in two days. Placements include entry-level office jobs at hospitals, universities, law firms, and private businesses.

Students' earned income goes directly to the school to help cover the costs of a Cristo Rey education. Typically businesses pay between $20,000 to $30,000 for each full-time job filled by a student team. That covers 40-60 percent of each student's school costs. Through their jobs, students are thus the biggest donors to Cristo Rey.

But the work-study program isn't just about money. It also gives low-income students real-life work experience in different kinds of office work, generally at top corporations and major businesses. This demystifies professional occupations for students who have often had little exposure to them, builds confidence, and imparts practical understanding and inspiration for further education.

Jane Genster, the president of the Cristo Rey Network, explains that work-study "was originally conceived as only a funding device. We quickly learned, however, that the work experience also contributes powerfully to our students' education, formation, and preparation for college and careers. They learn technological competence, attention to detail and directions, thorough research and clear writing, organization and presentation skills, and overall time management."

In recent years, Cristo Rey has captured national attention for its great success and rapid expansion. Educational experts have praised the ability of work-study programs to produce skills like teamwork, grit, and perseverance. In her 2014 book *Putting Education to Work: How Cristo Rey High Schools Are Transforming Urban Education*, journalist Megan Sweas admires the school network's entire approach. She praises Cristo Rey's rigorous coursework, and its well-developed character education, in addition to the positive influence of the work-study program.

Fully 96 percent of Cristo Rey's students are minorities, and their average family income is $34,000. Yet in recent years almost every single Cristo Rey graduate has been admitted to a two- or four-year college. Since 2009, Cristo Rey has partnered with 46 colleges and universities to offer counseling, guidance, and significant financial-aid packages that help its graduates succeed on campus. Cristo Rey's college graduation rate is currently double the level of students from similar backgrounds who attend other high schools.

> Fully 96 percent of Cristo Rey's students are minorities, and their average family income is $34,000. Yet 100 percent were accepted to a two- or four-year college.

In addition to its dramatic impact on student lives, Cristo Rey is transforming neighborhoods. And it is helping illuminate national discussions on education reform. Cristo Rey officials seek to use its success to show what Catholic schooling can offer to students from disadvantaged backgrounds.

Cristo Rey has expanded rapidly from its initial school to 30 schools in 19 states plus D.C. As this is written, six additional schools are in development in Baton Rouge, Dallas, Milwaukee, Philadelphia, Phoenix, and Tampa. Eleven more locations across the country have been targeted, with schools to open as philanthropic support allows. And as Genster puts it, "experience tells us that the integration of our rigorous college-prep academic curriculum with our distinctive work-study program uniquely equips our students for success in their post graduate lives."

Faith in the Future

Since 2009, a number of new networks of Catholic schools have launched. The Faith in the Future Foundation is one. It emerged in 2012 as an independent nonprofit to which the Archdiocese of Philadelphia ceded operational and financial responsibility for 17 high schools and four special-ed schools.

"Catholic schools are the best platform to create low-cost, high-quality education that forms productive citizens of real character," says foundation

CEO Casey Carter. "What we need to do is create a business model for these schools to thrive." The change of management control was crucial. "You have to change the governance structure first in order to create a new operating and business model," says Carter.

Under the initial five-year agreement, the archdiocese Office for Catholic Education that previously oversaw the schools became a division of the foundation and reports directly to the CEO. It remains responsible for curriculum and standards, guides academic and spiritual development of the students, and manages professional development of teachers. Business systems, fundraising, marketing, capital improvements, and expansion are the foundation's responsibility.

The Office of Catholic Education also continues to oversee the more than 100 Catholic schools throughout greater Philadelphia that continue to be owned and operated by parishes. While FIFF does not operate these schools directly, it provides them with ongoing support and guidance. Casey is focused on improving enrollment and modernizing enrollment systems; professionalizing fundraising; improving the quality of teachers and principals; enhancing educational and artistic programs; and deploying technology to measure, monitor, and drive improvements.

"We find economies of scale and create central services to support our schools," explains Ed Hanway, former chairman of Cigna Insurance and founder of the Faith in the Future Foundation. The organization has agreed to cover all operational deficits of its 21 schools. The foundation will raise money for this purpose from multiple sources: regional philanthropies, individuals, alumni, and the Pennsylvania tax-credit scholarship program.

Enrollment growth will be one of main ways the foundation intends to improve the economics of their schools, and good things are already happening on this front. "This year," said Carter in 2015, "we're expecting population gains of at least one percent, and it is largest among freshman and sophomores." The schools have also already increased their annual donations, thanks to improved fundraising processes. A networkwide $6 million deficit has been turned into a $1.2 million surplus.

Notre Dame ACE Academies

Since 1993 the Alliance for Catholic Education at the University of Notre Dame has been a leader in creating new ways of supporting Catholic schools. The ACE Teaching Fellows program has trained more than 1,200 high-quality teachers to serve in under-resourced Catholic schools, and its Mary Ann Remick Leadership Program has prepared more than 230 principals to lead them. (Both programs are described in more detail in Chapter 4.)

In 2005, leaders at ACE recognized that Catholic colleges need to offer even more assistance to Catholic schools. "Notre Dame serves the church in the U.S.," says Christian Dallavis of ACE. "If there's no Catholic K–12 system, then there's no Notre Dame. We need to do whatever we can to strengthen K–12. It has to be a part of our mission."

ACE began to expand rapidly in 2006. By 2010 it offered four degree and certificate programs specifically for Catholic educators, five outreach initiatives, and five services programs—one of which is Notre Dame ACE Academies. "Through ACE Academies," explains Dallavis, "we're trying to demonstrate that given the right governance structure and

> If there's no Catholic K-12 system, then there's no Notre Dame.

choice policies, Catholic schools serving low-income families can sustainably provide high-quality education and faith formation.

When ACE Academies goes into any diocese, an independent board is formed and the bishop yields authority over academics, operations, and finances for some of his schools to this board and ACE. This governance model ensures that the board, local pastors, and principals have clearly delegated responsibilities, but that they work together collaboratively.

ACE choose sites carefully, looking first and foremost for willing partners. "We look at the area's school-choice environment," explains Dallavis, "and at church leadership to make sure they are open to change. Our first two locations we were essentially invited in. We're not looking to antagonize or set up shop where we're not wanted."

ACE Academies provides support to partner schools in three main areas:

- *Catholic identity:* Building a strong school culture that sees "God in all things."
- *Growth:* Helping schools with financial management, marketing, and taking advantage of tax-credit and voucher programs.
- *Teaching:* Developing stronger teachers and principals.

The first three ACE Academies were established in 2010 in Tucson, Arizona, at the invitation of the local bishop. In 2012, the bishop in

St. Petersburg, Florida, invited ACE to partner with two schools in the Tampa Bay area. Both sites serve students in grades pre-K through 8, and accept students who qualify for state tax-credit scholarships. Combined, these five schools serve about 1,250 students.

The affiliation with Notre Dame is a major benefit. "We can bring some things to the schools that a standalone nonprofit couldn't," said Dallavis. "Our schools in Tucson now have Notre Dame's name plastered on their sides, and the city has a core of older Notre Dame alumni. So we have 70-year-old men who play golf in the morning and then spend the rest of the afternoon tutoring kids. Retired businessmen and engineers sit in classrooms with our ACE kids on a side of town they otherwise never would have gone to."

Since becoming an ACE Academy in 2010, St. John the Evangelist School in Tucson has experienced 91 percent enrollment growth. In 2010 its third-grade class scored in the 17th percentile nationally in math. Three years later, as fifth graders, these same children were in the 52nd percentile, surpassing the national average.

Notre Dame is expanding to new sites. In April of 2015, the university announced creation of four new ACE Academies in Orlando, Kissimmee, and Daytona Beach, Florida. "Our dream is that ACE Academies become the proof points for private and religious school choice that KIPP, Achievement First, and Success Academies have been for the charter-school movement," says Dallavis. "We want to be what people think of when they think of successful voucher schools."

Independence Mission Schools

Prior to 2010, St. Martin de Porres School faced challenges common to too many urban Catholic schools: declining enrollment, skyrocketing costs, growing debt, and the fear of closure. The school is located in an economically depressed neighborhood of North Philadelphia. It has served poor and minority families for over 100 years; today, 99 percent of the school's 400 students are black and many come from families living below the poverty line. But thanks to creative and generous business leaders and philanthropists (including construction entrepreneur Jack Donnelly, chairman of the school's board), St. Martin de Porres has rebounded. Indeed, the successful approach used to save this campus has paved the way for preservation of a whole string of threatened schools.

Back in 1980 a group of Philadelphians created Business Leaders Organized for Catholic Schools to help low-income children get religious education in their city. By 2014–2015 BLOCS was raising more than $10 million and granting partial scholarships to 5,500 students throughout greater Philadelphia. In 2010 the charity announced a new initiative in support of Catholic schools. Local philanthropists Gerry Lenfest and Michael O'Neill organized a $4 million matching grant to help seven schools create endowments that would bolster their long-term sustainability. Principals at the seven schools—of which St. Martin de Porres was one—agreed to raise $7 million within three years to qualify for the BLOCS bonus.

St. Martin de Porres hit its goal with the help of a funders auxiliary. Success led to agreement from the archdiocese that this charitable auxiliary, the Friends of St. Martin de Porres School, would assume leadership, operational, and financial responsibility for the high school. Philadelphia's Bishop Timothy Senior called the agreement "a future model for the success of our inner-city Catholic schools." Today, an 18-member board manages the school, while the archdiocese provides the curriculum.

In 2012, the archdiocese announced that it would be closing four high schools and 44 elementary schools (on the heels of 30 closures over the previous five years) due to declining enrollment and falling revenue. Schools were offered an appeals process that gave them a chance to demonstrate that they could remain open in some reorganized state, and as a result 18 elementary schools were granted reprieves. Archbishop Charles Chaput explained that "we are pleased to be working with Catholic community leaders who have stepped forward at a critical time."

Some philanthropic local businessmen came together to create a nonprofit capable of running high-quality Catholic schools in the city's neediest communities. The Independence Mission Schools organization ultimately took over operation of 15 Philadelphia Catholic schools. Their agreement with the archdiocese cedes the 15 campuses to them in perpetuity—on the condition that they continue to be operated as Catholic schools. The schools continue to receive support from the archdiocese's Office of Catholic Schools, but IMS has the authority to make any changes to curriculum or operations that its board deems necessary. Each school also signed onto the agreement individually, making it relatively easy, legally, to add additional schools in the future.

Closely modeled after the independent board at St. Martin de Porres, each IMS school now has its own advisory board. The umbrella organization provides operational support that improves academics and minimizes costs. "We've been able to grow enrollment in these schools

Close-up on Independence Mission Schools

During a period when enrollment at Philadelphia's diocese schools was dropping more than 30 percent, DePaul Catholic School ended up with just 181 students. Music instructors, physical-education teachers, and librarians had been cut, leaving the nine homeroom teachers juggling multiple responsibilities. Nearly half of the school's classrooms were unused.

When Independence Mission Schools took over eight campuses slated to be closed by the archdiocese, DePaul and five others opted to join their network. By 2015, three years later, there are a total of 15 affiliated schools and turnarounds are underway. DePaul has 485 students and is running out of classroom space. The school received 422 new applicants for the 2014-2015 school year.

IMS has lowered tuition every year, with the ultimate goal of bringing it under $2,000 per year as its fundraising gets more and more robust. It also handles enrollment from its headquarters office instead of letting this fall on overworked school staff as in the past.

Communication with parents has improved, and less than 1 percent of families are behind on their tuition across the IMS network. "There is greater transparency now," says IMS president Anne McGoldrick. "Parents know exactly where their money is going."

DePaul entered a cooperative agreement with Seton Education Partners in 2013 that is turning the school into a blended-learning campus. Use of sophisticated computer instruction allows a higher student-teacher ratio without sacrificing academic performance, saving costs while also personalizing instruction much more closely to each individual student. Every DePaul student now has a laptop and rotates between direct teacher instruction, group work with other students, and individual work at a computer. Teachers supervise small groups of students within the rotation model.

On the day of our visit, one third of the students in the second-grade classroom were working with scissors and glue, one third were doing math exercises on computers, and one third were taking a reading test. Students at the laptop stations had on headphones and were focused on their individual work. The students involved in the craft project had direct teacher supervision. She asked them questions about what they were assembling and they all shouted "no!" in unison.

Blended-learning software gives teachers and parents rich data on individual student progress and task mastery. "Blended learning challenges students at both ends of the spectrum," explained one teacher. "It builds confidence for struggling students, and offers new challenges to those who finish early. Everyone sees success at some point." Reading growth at DePaul has been significant since the new instruction began: the number of K-2 students reading on grade level increased by 42 percent in four months.

The IMS network has made it easier for teachers in its Catholic schools to get involved in useful peer networks like PhillyPLUS, KIPP's Emerging Leader Program, and offerings of the Philadelphia School Partnership. For instance, four school leaders have completed the PhillyPlus fellowship, described as "career changing," and four more will do so this coming year. PhillyPlus works with about 20 teachers at a time, from district-run, charter, religious, and private schools, who aspire to school-leadership positions. The two-year program provides training in year one, then helps place fellows in management positions and provides coaching and support throughout year two. Connections like this with experts and other teachers are helping Catholic educators thrive. "We know whom to call when we have questions," says IMS's McGoldrick. "This would have been like manna from heaven for a standalone Catholic school."

Rising enrollment and improved finances have enabled a number of IMS campuses to hire an assistant principal. McGoldrick describes these additions as "the best investment" they've made. "We were asking people to turn things around and then we actually gave them the resources to do so." Before IMS, only two schools had assistant principals; at the start of the 2015-2016 school year, there will be nine.

IMS is hiring higher quality, more experienced staff attracted by the renewed mission for these schools. It has also been able to reduce teacher turnover significantly at all schools. The organization needs time to develop stronger teacher-evaluation systems, but in the meantime they are offering more professional development to instructors and leaders. One principal, for instance, will attend the highly successful Relay Graduate School of Education beginning this summer. Teachers are being trained for new work in summer literacy programs and on a blended-learning initiative.

The new management structure is allowing staff to focus on instruction, curricular updates, and new teaching styles. At St. Thomas Aquinas School, for example, a recent grant funded the school's first science lab, with digital microscopes and a hands-on curriculum aligned with Common Core standards. Small group instruction is a new emphasis. Evidence of increased student engagement can be seen in improved daily attendance rates.

As in many inner-city Catholic schools, a significant majority of the students in the Independence Mission Schools are not Catholic. Yet the network is committed to offering spiritual education that is relevant to Catholics and non-Catholics alike. Prayer services include students of all Christian faiths. All campuses have religious icons in the hallways. Walls are peppered with inspirational statements from religious figures.

"Christ is the reason for this school" reads one sign at DePaul.

Important questions remain: How many non-Catholic teachers and principals would IMS hire? Are there key roles that should always be staffed by Catholics? The network is still working out these issues, but it is clear the education being offered remains a Catholic one. "The world constantly tells these kids that they don't have value. We tell them they do, that they are all creatures in God's love," says McGoldrick. The choice to keep the original Catholic name of each school also honors the importance of the neighborhood's history and its intangible social capital.

Donors considering importing elements of the Independence Mission Schools approach to other cities should be aware of two details that helped this network spring up. Pennsylvania has a small tax-credit scholarship program that allows some families to afford tuition that would otherwise be beyond reach. (Such programs are discussed in Chapter 5.) And when the archdiocese handed over its schools to the nonprofit, it ceded practically all control, allowing the board of directors to innovate and find new solutions. This autonomy will be central to the healthy evolution of these schools.

in a way that just wasn't possible before, and teachers and principals have a whole new level of resources at their disposal," notes IMS president Anne McGoldrick. "This is only our second year but already I'm sensing better energy and morale. Our leaders and teachers have an appetite for change. People are getting excited by new approaches."

Every single IMS student comes from a low-income family; 64 percent are African-American and 13 percent are Hispanic; 100 percent attend the school on financial aid. These students pay tuition, but private philanthropy and state tax-credit scholarships are crucial to meeting annual school costs of $4,500 per student per year.

Partnership for Inner-city Education

In 2011, the Archdiocese of New York reconfigured its Catholic schools from a traditional parish-based system to a regional system. Whether they had a school or not, all parishes would contribute financially to support the schools in the area. Each Catholic-school region was set up as a separate educational nonprofit chartered by the New York State Department of Education. In each region, a board of trustees that mixes church officials and laity is appointed to manage all aspects of the schools.

This spinoff allowed further, even more localized, devolutions of Catholic schools to take place in particular neighborhoods. "We can't afford 'business as usual'. We need to try new administrative models to address the challenges faced by Catholic education today and to ensure our schools thrive and stay strong for future generations," said New York Cardinal Timothy Dolan in 2013. So at that same time, six inner-city schools in Harlem and the Bronx were placed under the management of a donor group called the Partnership for Inner-city Education. The archdiocese retains ownership of the school facilities and oversees the religious curriculum, but the Partnership has broad authority over most remaining aspects of school operation.

Philanthropist Russ Carson, a longtime supporter of Catholic schools and now the Partnership's board chairman, found that giving in the form of scholarships wasn't improving Catholic schools as he'd hoped and that he could contribute more by helping set up an independent school operator like the Partnership. "Russ wanted to start it with just a few schools to see if it could work," says Partnership director Jill Kafka. The group studied charter-school operators "to see how they staff their central office—what they centralize, what they don't."

The Partnership allocated $9 million to improve buildings, buy new classroom materials, train teachers, and launch new enrichment programs for students. Once they have fully ramped up, these six schools aim to serve more than 2,000 students (the vast majority of whom come from low-income families). That growth will only happen, the leadership team understands, if student results are excellent. "The goal is to get the same results as the best charters in the neighborhood," says Kafka. "Strong academics will raise enrollment, and full enrollment will stabilize finances."

"We have effective control of the schools. We have the right to hire and fire the principals, the right to change the academic components of the schools. We have full responsibility for the educational product that we are now delivering," noted Carson in a recent discussion with other donors sponsored by FADICA, a group that assists Catholic-school funders. "In return for this we've devoted significant dollars to fixing up the schools and adding additional programs and capabilities. At some point, we will have to step up our outside fundraising. And that will be totally dependent on our ability to demonstrate that we have materially raised the educational quality of the schools."

The governance issue we've been exploring in this chapter was front and center when the negotiations took place to create the Partnership for Inner-city Education. "Our deal with the archdiocese has gone very smoothly so far," says Carson, but "at the very beginning, the cardinal was concerned about turning over control of the schools. So we countered that by adding a clause that allows the archdiocese to terminate at any time. And the partnership can terminate at any time if we aren't happy with the way the archdiocese is treating the schools. That's been a very effective measure to keep both sides honest."

Lessons from other private schools

Supporters and managers of Catholic education can also learn many useful things from the experiences of other religious and private schools. Following are three private-school operations that may offer lessons.

The Oaks Academy

The first campus of Oaks Academy was founded by a small group of neighbors who envisioned an excellent Christ-centered education for students living in inner-city Indianapolis. In 1998 the school welcomed 53 students into classrooms offering grades K-8. A second K-5 location was launched in 2011. By 2015, those two campuses served more than 600 students, and a third campus—the chain's dedicated middle school—was opening.

Director of advancement Nathan Hand describes Oaks as "one school in three locations. We have a singular philosophy and mission across all of our locations." This focus on a narrow, non-negotiable shared culture is common among successful school chains. The connective tissue within these networks of schools is more than a name or a common finance system, it's also values and mission.

Bringing their education to an ever-widening circle of families is a priority for Oaks leaders, and they have a carefully developed expansion model that works much like the way evangelical Christians plant churches: "We incubate families at the original campus for a year and then send them to launch the second model," states Hand. "These families soak up the model and become pioneers at the new campus. We also identify teachers and leaders who really get us, and ask them to move to the next campus. We want to launch the same school each time."

> The cardinal was concerned about turning over control of the schools. So we countered that by adding a clause that allows the archdiocese to terminate at any time.

This approach has been successful at transferring the school's culture, though Hand acknowledges challenges: "The sending school had to reckon with beloved teachers leaving and being replaced by new teachers." Donors should be mindful of this perennial challenge of replication. The only way to reliably spread culture is through people. But shifting people from one location to another comes at a price.

The Oaks Academy prides itself on its racial and socioeconomic diversity. Half of enrolled students come from low-income families, one quarter come from middle-income families, and one quarter come from higher-income families. The school maintains a roughly equal proportion of African-American and white students.

The three schools rely on a mixed funding model. Fifty percent of the network's income comes from family-paid tuition. Philanthropy covers about 30 percent of the overall budget. And Indiana's private-school voucher program covers about 20 percent of costs. "Everyone pays something," remarks Hand, but discounted rates make it possible for low-income families to afford tuition.

In addition to offering a Christ-centered education in a diverse environment, academic results at The Oaks are impressive. Ninety-five percent of students pass both the math and language sections of the state assessment. Those scores place it in the top 5 percent of schools in the state.

HOPE Christian Schools

HOPE Christian Schools is a network of six Christian schools in Wisconsin run by a nonprofit called Educational Enterprises Inc. The first HOPE school opened in 2002. Today the network operates five schools in Milwaukee and a sixth in Racine. In 2015, school reformers in Louisiana announced a $900,000 investment to open four new HOPE Christian Schools in Baton Rouge, the first grant from their Excellence Fund to be used for non-public schools.

Educational Enterprises Inc. is unusual in that it also runs a network of charter schools in Arizona and Missouri called Eagle College Prep. "We started with the Christian schools, not charter schools," explains EEI's Ciji Pittman. "We think the faith element is important. It's one of the three main gaps we believe our schools are filling—the racial achievement gap, the gap in forming character in young people, and the shortage of high-quality faith-based schools."

Without consistent public funding for religious and private schools, however, EEI considered charter schools the next-best option. "There was a community in St. Louis that really wanted a school like HOPE, but it just wasn't possible because the funding wasn't there. So we opened a charter school instead." Because the faith element is so important to EEI's mission, all of its charter schools offer a supplemental program called Compass that provides religious-education programming to students.

In Wisconsin, which has been a national star in treating religious and private schools fairly, EEI's HOPE Christian Schools for kindergarten through eighth-grade students have thrived. Although the children they enroll typically arrive scoring significantly below their district average on statewide math and reading tests, after attending HOPE for two years, the typical student outscores district peers in both subjects.

HOPE's financial model depends heavily on Wisconsin's public funding. It also counts on about $750,000 of philanthropic support whenever they launch another school. Tuition payments, state vouchers, and this initial philanthropic funding "allow us to break even in year four or five. We don't open a new school unless it'll be sustainable on its own without ongoing support," explains Pittman.

When deciding where to expand, the availability of initial philanthropic support and of reliable state or city support for school-choice assistance are the two main elements leaders look for. Fair treatment from governments is the shakiest piece of this. Even in Wisconsin, with the nation's oldest voucher program, political struggles can squeeze private schools that rely on the program. "We were all set to open in Racine and the budget proposal came down with huge cuts," reports Pittman. "We were given assurances that this would be fixed, but we had to move forward with finding a facility and hiring leaders and teachers without clarity. The funding and policy are so unstable that it makes it really hard to rely on it."

Having successfully navigated these challenges, HOPE Christian Schools opened the 2015-2016 school year offering more than 2,000 students a high-quality, faith-based education. The organization's accomplishments offer insights for Catholic-school donors. In operating both religious schools and charter schools, it has mixed and matched strengths of each educational type. Its charter-school variant required effort to figure out what faith elements could be retained, and how. And the religious schools have learned to weather the ups and downs of public budgeting and politics that sometimes ruffle school-choice programs.

LUMIN

Concern over the loss of Lutheran schools in Milwaukee spurred a group of business leaders, educators, and financial backers of the Lutheran Church–Missouri Synod to launch LUMIN (the Lutheran Urban Mission Initiative) to support that city's struggling Lutheran schools. Between 2005 and 2009, four Milwaukee schools were rescued from financial pressures. In 2012 LUMIN re-opened a shuttered campus. And in 2014 the nonprofit took over a struggling academy in the city of Racine.

"All of the schools were distressed in one form or another," explains Richard Laabs, the group's president. "Once we turned them around and revived them financially, then we set our sights on growth and quality." Today, LUMIN operates six schools serving nearly 1,600 students in grades pre-K through 8.

LUMIN has a headquarters staff of about 20 employees divided into three teams. One oversees all business functions (accounting, finance, budgeting, facilities, human resources, marketing, etc.). A second manages academic aspects of the schools (curriculum, instruction, assessments, data collection, etc.). The third team orchestrates student and family services (counselors, social workers, health care, after-school, etc.).

Nearly all of LUMIN's 1,600 students are financially eligible for Wisconsin's voucher program, and like the HOPE Christian Schools, LUMIN relies heavily on the state payments. This influences its growth planning, as the network will only consider expanding into cities or states with sufficient and reliable private-school choice programs. LUMIN is currently exploring opportunities to expand into nearby Indiana—where an excellent private-school choice program exists.

"We've been relatively unsuccessful at raising philanthropic money," reports Laabs. "We have about six local foundations that support us. And one large national funder has been good to us, but they changed their direction and basically backed out. The grants we've obtained have mostly been used to fund startup schools or significant renovation projects. In some cases, we've used grants to fund a new position or a new initiative until we reach the scale to build it into our operating budget. But the voucher program is our lifeline."

To grow its network, LUMIN has expanded existing institutions as well as acquiring new schools. It has both started schools afresh and taken over existing campuses. In addition to having internal capacity, a school operator that wants to grow needs clear positive market signals, warns Laabs. "If you're going to open a new school, you'd better identify an underserved community versus one that's already saturated."

Due diligence on governance changes

There are many ways that donors can improve and sustain Catholic schools. The best options will vary depending on the community, and will be dictated by a combination of factors. These include the willingness of school and church leaders to change longstanding practices, the quality of the school's leadership, its trajectory over the latest decade, the nature of the families it has the potential to serve, the views of the families it currently serves, the possibilities of creating helpful partnerships, the cohesion of the local Catholic donor community, the presence of competing schools, the school-choice environment of the state, and so on.

In some contexts, encouraging the creation of relatively loose consortia may be enough. If more sharing of information and joint efficiency are the main things that are missing, then just bringing existing schools together to share lessons and resources, and incentivizing leaders to tinker with new approaches—as the Specialty Family Foundation did in Los Angeles—may be enough. In other circumstances, however, wholly different governance structures may be necessary before donors begin pouring money into their Catholic schools.

Because most Catholic-education donors have been loyally involved with their local schools for years, they will often already have a sophisticated understanding of the complexities of these schools. But before launching any serious intervention it may be wise to refresh one's store of information on topics like these:

- Past and current enrollment trends, and future projections
- A nuanced picture of academic outcomes and how they compare to surrounding and peer institutions
- An accurate profile of the existing teaching and principal force
- An understanding of the schools' philanthropic history, including key donors, successful initiatives, and failures
- School facility needs
- School and system-level financial status
- Adequacy of prevailing business and marketing practices
- A good read on the local church leadership

Once donors have a solid understanding of these important details, they should swiftly turn their attention to the mechanics of change. Transforming century-old institutions can be complicated, especially if there are not strong leaders on the other side of the table. Without enthusiasm and commitment to making a leap forward, negotiations on spinning off schools into new governance can bog down on details.

Donors must have confidence that their partners are not going to get hung up on whether the school gets to use the church parking lot. Things that matter, like what gets spent on building repairs, and the size of diocese subsidies for parishioners' tuition, either need to be established in advance, or be rendered moot by the schools' operational autonomy. Vital aspects of autonomy can be negotiated before donors take responsibility for their groups of schools—as was done by the Catholic Partnership in Camden, or Faith in the Future in Philadelphia, or the Partnership for Inner-city Education in New York City—or it can be grasped by creating a new entity from scratch, like in the case of the Cristo Rey schools.

It's worth remembering that large governance changes can have large transaction costs (community resistance, friction from church or school staff, and so forth). Donors must be sure what they win is worth the effort expended. In some cases a simple memorandum of understanding might accomplish all that is needed, without ruffling feathers about who owns what, and who is ultimately in charge. In other instances, a thoroughgoing change of control and management may be essential if school performance and sustainability are to be dramatically improved.

Donors should consider the human element in these projects, not just what the data say. Many people interpret change, especially fundamental change, as an indictment of their previous work. Even inadequate work is sometimes associated with self-sacrificing effort. To avoid backlashes, change management that helps people understand what is happening and why it is necessary should be part of any major reform. "We have to remember that we're dealing with people and culture and existing communities," summarizes Anne McGoldrick of Independence Mission Schools. "We need to bring them along, not necessarily slowly but carefully, so they can embrace the change."

Once donors have a full picture of their local school landscape and the challenges facing it, they might ask themselves questions like these:

• What are the most pressing problems that need to be solved?
• What are the ultimate sources of these problems?
• Can governance responsibilities be adjusted to solve existing problems?
• Or is new governance needed?
• Is church and school leadership willing to contemplate disruptive change?
• Who must be involved, and in what ways, for this to work?

Faith-inspired charter schools

Donors have options that are even bolder than making big changes in the governance of existing Catholic schools. One newer approach to expanding (and altering) the influence of Catholic schooling is to open "faith-inspired" charter schools. These schools are often housed in buildings once occupied by religious schools. They integrate many of the values and pedagogical approaches of faith-based schools. They typically offer religious programming outside of the normal school day. Importantly, though, they can neither explicitly teach religion nor affiliate with a particular religious denomination—because as public schools, charters must avoid heavy church-state entanglements prohibited by the Constitution.

The Catalyst Schools in Chicago are examples of faith-inspired charter schools that grew out of Catholic education. Beginning around 2000, Paul Vallas, head of the Chicago Public Schools, began asking the

Christian Brothers, who run the successful San Miguel Catholic schools in his city, to open a charter school for the district. For six years, the Brothers said no, first to Vallas and then to his successor Arne Duncan.

Then in 2006 the Brothers agreed. "We finally got to a point where we felt compelled to respond," explains Catalyst Schools co-founder Ed Siderewicz. "We knew we had a gift and that Arne recognized that gift. It became about doing something completely new that was bigger than us, something that would be good for humanity and for society. We thought we could bring the best from the private Catholic-school model to public education today, and do it with authenticity and integrity while still respecting the law of the land."

Catalyst's two schools serve populations that are nearly 100 percent black and low-income. Nonetheless, 90 percent of its seniors graduated in 2013. This compares to 75 percent of students nationally and 63 percent of Chicago Public Schools students.

As public institutions, the Catalyst charter schools cannot provide religious instruction during the school day. Instead, they were founded on four core values that closely align to the values of the Catholic San Miguel schools: relationships, results, rigor, and hope. Students are taught their inherent value as human beings and are instructed to value relationships with fellow man. Siderewicz likens the Catalyst teachers to "urban missionaries" who "believe in these children, in their value, and in their potential to make a difference in the world."

Catalyst also offers religious wraparound programming through the Maria Kaupas Center. The center provides Catholic instruction for Catalyst students after school. Special efforts are made to reach Catalyst's students of high-school age.

Siderewicz understands the discomfort many feel about the perceived lack of "Catholicness" in these schools. After all, it took him six years to say yes to this project. No matter how "inspired" a faith-inspired charter school may be, practically speaking it does lose much of its distinctiveness when talking to children about God is put off limits.

Siderewicz acknowledges this, yet points out that "only about one in 10 students can afford Catholic schools today, and that's a problem that's not being dealt with fast enough. What we're doing is the most Catholic thing we can think of to do given the financial circumstances of Catholic schools. We're finding a way to serve those who would otherwise be overlooked. It's a disservice to God's children to not do anything, to just keep hoping that things will get better."

He insists that supporting Catholic schools and opening faith-inspired charter schools isn't an either/or decision: "We're not trying to replace Catholic schools. Where Catholic schools are thriving and can continue, they *must* continue. They're national treasures and beacons of hope for thousands of children in underserved communities. But where they're struggling, there needs to be a very real conversation about how to fix that. It has to be both/and."

In addition to a safe, high-quality education, Catalyst Schools aims to provide hope to children living in difficult communities. The school has established partnerships with local faith-based institutions, which have been vital to the success of the schools and students. Network leaders are contemplating new campuses (possibly in different cities), as well as conversions of Catholic schools (see next section). But these decisions have not been finalized.

For Siderewicz, one of the greatest markers of success has been watching skepticism and doubt turn to hope as people actually experience the schools. "We had a benefactor breakfast last week," he recounts. "One stakeholder said, 'It feels like a public Catholic school to me.'"

Catholic-school conversions

Decidedly more controversial than starting new faith-infused charter schools is to take existing, financially struggling Catholic schools and convert them to charter status. One of the best-known examples of "sector switching" occurred in Washington, D.C. In the late 1990s, declining enrollment in the city's Catholic elementary system led the diocese to recommend the closure of numerous schools. Instead, Cardinal Hickey and his team created a new central office to take on administrative tasks, freeing principals and pastors of many pressing needs at the threatened schools. The office became known as the Center City Consortium. Consortium staff focused on preserving the 12 endangered schools and ensuring their quality. Though the consortium raised $60 million between 1997 and 2007, financial challenges continued. The consortium faced a $7 million deficit in the 2007-08 school year, and a projected $56 million shortfall over the ensuing five years.

In 2007, a new plan was drafted: keep four schools that were in the best shape operating in a smaller consortium of Catholic schools and convert the other eight into a new network of charter schools. Ultimately, one of the eight slated for charter conversion submitted a sustainability plan that was approved, and it was allowed to become a standalone parish-sponsored Catholic school. The remaining seven were converted to charter schools.

The rationale for this plan was simple: As charters, the seven schools would be eligible for public funding. And the schools would remain open in the same buildings, with many of the same teachers, staff, and students—providing a considerable degree of stability for students who would otherwise be displaced by a closure. The downside was also clear: The schools would be unable to teach the Catholic faith in their new form. Many advocates believe that the unusual ability of Catholic schools to lead difficult populations to academic and life success, despite having far fewer resources than public schools, is a direct product of their religious mission, which therefore cannot be put aside.

This same concern pressed on leaders and stakeholders in the Archdiocese of Miami as they contemplated a 2009 plan to close seven Catholic schools and open eight public charter schools in the newly empty buildings. That course of action was eventually followed, and ultimately judged a success by some observers (who were pleased that it gave parish priests a source of income, through renting their school buildings, to pay off past debts to the archdiocese and others and thereby sustain their parishes). As in D.C., this course also gave the children who had been attending the Catholic schools a better option than being thrown into conventional public schools of a low quality.

Blended learning

Blended learning combines direct instruction from a teacher, plus small-group activities, with computerized instruction that is personalized for the student depending on how quickly he or she masters a topic. It has been shown to be a powerful tool, particularly for underprivileged children. And because there is some substitution of technology for expensive teachers, it can also help schools save money—offering win-win possibilities for Catholic institutions struggling to keep their tuition affordable.

Teachers can incorporate blended learning into their classrooms in a variety of formats and instructional approaches. Whole systems or schools may choose to adopt a blended model, or individual teachers may implement blended-learning programs in particular classrooms. The Philanthropy Roundtable's recent book *Blended Learning: A Wise Giver's Guide to Supporting Tech-assisted Teaching* provides lots of background and detail on the bright educational prospects of blended learning.

Blended-learning models carry significant up-front costs. To implement high-quality programs, schools must acquire computers, software, high-volume Internet connections, and teacher training. Donors are indispensable for schools making these initial investments. Once the initial financial hurdles have been jumped, there is promising evidence that blended learning may save schools money in the long run. A recent report by the Fordham Institute finds that the national average cost per pupil per year for a traditional brick-and-mortar school is $10,000, while schools employing blended learning fall between $7,600 and $10,200.

There is promising evidence that blended learning may save schools money at the same time it improves student performance.

In addition to potential savings, blended learning makes it easier for Catholic schools to meet diverse needs among their students. The low-income, minority students that attend many urban Catholic schools often arrive with significant learning delays, gaps in their knowledge, and need for individualized attention to get them caught up. Blended learning is excellent at uncovering and then filling in such gaps. In reading and math especially, high-quality software exists that enables students to learn material at their own pace while providing teachers with frequent assessments of where each student is progressing and where he or she is stuck.

Technology can provide schools with access to rich content that their limited budgets would otherwise not allow. For example, Catholic schools often want to offer students foreign-language classes, but recruiting qualified teachers can be a challenge, and small schools can often afford only one— yielding just a single foreign-language option. A computerized language lab, however, can provide good instruction in many tongues at reasonable cost.

Here are some promising blended-learning models now being implemented in Catholic schools across the country:

Seton Education Partners

Seton Education Partners is a nonprofit offering services to urban Catholic schools across the country. It has created a blended-learning curriculum that inner-city Catholic schools can use to prepare their students to be competitive with more advantaged peers.

"We've seen many schools try to implement blended learning on their own, and despite great intentions, too many fail to fundamentally change the way learning happens in the classroom, which is what blended learning is best for," says Seton co-founder Stephanie Saroki de Garcia. "At each of our partner schools we select and train a full-time blended-learning manager (always someone who's had success with underserved children as a teacher). We ensure that children learn every little routine—from what to do when they get stuck, to how to do short rotations so no learning time is lost. We pay attention to the non-technical aspects of great learning—especially relationships and motivation—so we can enhance the very things that have traditionally made Catholic schools successful."

Seton piloted its blended-learning methods at the Mission Dolores Academy in San Francisco, starting in 2011. Students there receive blended-learning instruction in math, English, social studies, and science. In each class, students rotate on a fixed schedule between computer stations and face-to-face direct or small-group instruction with the teacher. Students spend approximately one third of their class time, or approximately 80 minutes per day, using online learning software.

Seton has since expanded this blended-learning model to schools in Los Angeles, Philadelphia, Cincinnati, Milwaukee, and New Orleans. Seton now supports eight schools in its six cities, using blended learning to both improve the academic progress of students and cut per pupil costs. Success has been realized in both areas.

First finances: At Mission Dolores Academy, the new blended-learning methods allowed the school to move from a 14:1 student-teacher ratio to a 25:1 ratio. That reduced per-pupil costs from $15,000 to below $10,000 in the first year.

Academic performance is also improving. Students in Seton's blended-learning schools take a national achievement test every year. In the 2014–2015 school year, 78 percent of them made at least a year's worth of growth in math, and 72 percent did so in reading. The national average is 50 percent. This academic growth is even better than what is achieved on the same test at most high-performing charter schools.

"We're impressed by the results so far and excited about the opportunities to take academic performance even higher," reports principal Dan Stortz. "The students like the immediate feedback. And teachers report that students are more engaged and classrooms are easier to manage with the activity rotation and smaller group instruction." Parents also seem pleased. The schools that have shifted to Seton's blended-learning model have experienced an average enrollment growth of 30 percent.

Blended learning, says Seton co-founder Scott Hamilton, "creates time and space for small-group instruction, giving teachers more opportunities to meet the particular needs of each student." Instructional talent remains important. "We don't hire anyone to work with kids unless we've assessed their teaching, have evidence of student-achievement results, and really get to know them in a series of interviews and exercises," says Saroki de Garcia.

But she repeated a refrain we have heard many times: Catholic education is struggling to find and keep all the excellent teachers and leaders it needs. "Virtually no one in the country is recruiting, selecting, and compensating urban Catholic-school leaders the right way. In one of our blended-learning sites we're working with a great principal and he's getting paid $50,000 to do one of the toughest jobs in America. He is not going to stay."

Catholic schools need better ways of producing and retaining gifted educators. That is the subject of our next chapter. But by reducing the sheer number of good teachers needed, and by making decent teachers even better, blending learning helps bridge the talent gap.

If Seton's blended learning is to continue to spread, significant support from philanthropists will be required. Depending on their size, schools need $400,000 or more for hardware, software, wiring, and training in order to shift to the program. To date, donors like the Walton, Hilton, Peters, Bradley, and Specialty foundations and the Philadelphia School Partnership have been vital partners in bringing blended learning to Catholic schools.

San Jose Drexel Initiative

Located in booming Santa Clara County, the schools of the Catholic diocese of San Jose have mostly avoided the dramatic enrollment losses and financial strains experienced by schools in many other big cities. Even so, five of their schools were beginning to experience enrollment decline by 2012, as free charter schools pulled away students. Rather than wait for things to reach a crisis point, church leaders took action. "We must seize this moment to usher in a period of growth and stability," Bishop Patrick McGrath concluded, "not simply manage a period of maintenance or decline."

Inspired by the success of blended learning with poor children at

Seton's nearby Mission Dolores Academy, the diocese created its Saint Katharine Drexel Initiative in 2013. This brings blended learning to seven elementary schools. Students at these schools use iPads and other technology to guide their personalized instruction.

From the outset, the Drexel Initiative had two purposes: to improve student learning and to help the schools financially. Schools superintendent Kathy Almazol says the thing they most wanted from the new technology was to "increase student engagement and learning."

While modeled on Seton's approach—students in Drexel Initiative

> Virtually no one in the country is recruiting, selecting, and compensating urban Catholic-school leaders the right way.

classrooms rotate in small groups between online and face-to-face instruction—the Drexel Initiative has its own distinctive aspects. These schools remain part of the existing Catholic system, but administrative and financial responsibility for the schools was shifted upward, from the parish to the diocese.

"We changed the governance model to allow priests to do what they are trained to do, which is provide pastoral care," says the Reverend Brendan McGuire, a former Silicon Valley technology executive and now a diocese official. "I want less of their time spent on administration and more of their time in the classroom and in the schoolyard, because that's where they have the biggest impact. I worked in the corporate world and I worked really, really hard, but I can tell you it pales in comparison to how much I work right now. And that's the biggest problem facing pastors."

A second distinctive aspect of the Drexel schools is their partnership with nearby Santa Clara University. "About 10 years ago SCU developed a Catholic School Leadership program, and our schools have benefited greatly from the leaders that have come through there," says Almazol. Now SCU provides training and a blended-learning certificate program to all of the Drexel teachers.

Local philanthropist John Sobrato, whose company has built many of the commercial structures in Silicon Valley, was a crucial contributor to the Drexel Initiative from the beginning. "We were looking to do something different and exciting. Sobrato was involved. The university got involved. The stars aligned and, with a lot of hard work, it all came together," Almazol summarizes.

Virtual schooling

Unlike blended learning where students continue to have face-to-face instructional time with a teacher and with other students in groups, virtual schools provide all of their content and instruction online from a remote location. While lots of virtual schools exist, the primary operator offering a specifically Catholic online experience is Catholic Schools K-12 Virtual. CSK12 is both its own freestanding, degree-granting virtual school, and a provider of online courses to traditional Catholic schools who want to supplement their offerings. Schools offer CSK12 classes for various purposes: as advanced courses, to extend their school day, as after-school programs, as summer school, or for students who need to make up credits after failing a class.

Courses are available for students in grades 3-12. They are offered in modules, allowing schools or individual families to create custom classes. Courses come with a syllabus and a guide to help students work through the material at their own pace. They are divided into 36 weekly units of five daily lessons, although the pace can be modified to match individual needs. Students can contact CSK12 teachers via e-mail or telephone, and book appointments for questions or special help. CSK12 also provides live tutorials that students can access through the organization's website.

WINGS

In 2009, three Catholic schools in small, rural communities in Michigan were slated to be consolidated together. They had enrollments of 26, 41, and 58 students respectively. But a poll of families revealed that parents would continue to enroll their children only if the consolidated school was located at their current campus. This meant that even if they were combined, the sustainability of the schools would remain doubtful. So church and community leaders developed a plan.

The result was the WINGS Satellite Initiative. School administration was reduced to one principal shared across the three campuses. The three separate school boards were melded into one expanded board. And technology was employed to effect a "virtual consolidation" of the three schools. Funding is still parish-based, with each parish responsible for the facility and faculty specific to its site.

A number of challenges had to be navigated for this to work, including staff layoffs, figuring out ways to combine children in new classroom structures, and training teachers in different teaching methods and new technology. Each satellite campus uses computer and individualized blended-learning instruction. And some classrooms combine students of multiple grade levels.

The schools faced a number of challenges in their first year. Bandwidth was not sufficient to support the new computer-based instruction, and some of the software did not work as planned. But by the second year most of the kinks had been worked out.

Combined enrollment across the three schools has increased from previous levels. And the consolidation allowed the schools to create a sustainable student–teacher ratio. Overall costs were reduced by nearly 17 percent (more than $150,000 annually), even while wider study opportunities became available at the remade schools.

Parish.Academy

Responding to the emergence of micro schools, the importance of controlling tuition costs, and the desire for Catholic education in places that might not be able to support a larger school, Parish.Academy offers a lean new operating alternative. Its model is designed to enroll a total of 40-160 students. It is built on a proprietary blended-learning curriculum and intended to fit in underutilized parish facilities, without dedicated administrators. Thanks to their computerized curriculum, Parish.Academy schools are projected to run on a $3,850 per-pupil budget, considerably lower than the average tuition rate of a Catholic school.

"A million-dollar donor could open four 160-student micro-schools in the first year, and then two more schools every year without additional investment or fundraising," says Parish.Academy CEO Gareth Genner. The use of blended learning also enables students to receive a more personalized education that fits their specific needs. Schools maintain their Catholic identity and take faith formation seriously, using Catholic mentors from the parish. While the model is just developing, Genner was chosen to go through the nationally recognized 4.0 Schools incubator, where he developed and honed all aspects of Parish.Academy. To ensure that the blended-learning curriculum works, the model was also successfully piloted in a New Orleans charter school.

Other models for Catholic-school reform

The varied demands of families, and wide interests of donors, create openings for other ways of reforming Catholic schools to make them more effective, attractive to parents, and financially sustainable. The future of the Sacred Heart of Jesus School in Grand Rapids, Michigan, for instance, was once in jeopardy. Then it was remade into a "classical" academy with a rigorous curriculum focused on the Western intellectual tradition.

Board president Dave Phelps described to us the crisis he and the Reverend Robert Sirico faced in 2013. "At my first board meeting, the first order of business was whether we should close the school. It was in a bad state. The principal was on his way out. Enrollment had been plummeting for years. There wasn't even a budget. There hadn't been a school board in years. The school had trouble collecting tuition. There had been a number of school closings in the diocese, so nobody would've blamed us if we decided to follow suit. But the decision was made to see this as an opportunity to do something radical. It was time to throw a Hail Mary, and if it didn't work, there wasn't much to lose."

Local leaders decided to re-found the school as Sacred Heart Academy with a revamped academic program focused on the long arc of Western culture. "By completely overhauling the curriculum into a classical model, we differentiated the school significantly from other options—Catholic and otherwise—in the city," Phelps explains. "We also opened our doors to homeschooling families to take a la carte classes. In the first year, enrollment grew half again with students taking advantage of this option."

"When we started, the school had 72 students. Now we serve over 240 kids." As a result, says Phelps, "the whole parish is going through a renaissance."

Back in 2010, the financially troubled St. Jerome School in Hyattsville, Maryland, adopted a similar approach prioritizing study of the arts, sciences, and literature starting with ancient Greek and Roman sources. It began to offer Latin, Greek history, logic, rhetoric, fine-arts history, traditional moral training, the Socratic method, poetry memorization, and other intellectual challenges to its elementary-age students. It is not located in a wealthy area, but its new offerings attracted a range of families, and applications soared almost immediately. The St. Jerome curriculum was soon adopted by other schools in New York, Kentucky, Colorado, and elsewhere, and sparked a Catholic classical movement that now holds annual conferences and offers many forms of support.

The highly successful, 19-campus charter-school chain known as Great Hearts Academies has shown that there is a strong appetite among parents for schools that provide traditional, classical liberal-arts education. Curricula combining classical education and Christian instruction are very popular among homeschooling families. The national Association of Classical & Christian Schools has close to 250 member schools, many of them thriving, but all but a handful have an evangelical Christian orientation. This is a niche that Catholic schools, particularly those with access to middle-class families, ought to be able to occupy successfully. Donors could make that happen in many cities.

One donor that has invested in several new approaches to Catholic schooling is the GHR Foundation of Minneapolis. "We support the testing and incubation of new models," says program officer Meg Gehlen Nodzon. "We need to do things differently in the future, including differentiating ourselves beyond just being Catholic."

GHR has a partnership with St. Catherine University that will soon launch a new STEM program at a Catholic school in St. Paul. They were preceded in this direction by Visitation Catholic STEM Academy in Tacoma, Washington. It represents a fascinating blend of the old and new, bringing a modern academic approach to a school in operation since 1925, and combining Catholic education's traditional moral and ethical instruction with a curriculum focused on science, technology, engineering, and math.

GHR also has a partnership with Boston College that is bringing to Minneapolis a "two-way language immersion" program that the college's Roche Center for Catholic Education has rolled out in 19 schools across the country. This will allow students to receive half of their instruction in English and half in Spanish. Similarly, the Escuela de Guadalupe School in Denver has gained national recognition for its successful dual-language program.

Fresh opportunities for savvy donors

Today's oft-seen willingness to alter, remake, or trade in what was once thought to be the immutable, defining characteristic of Catholic education—the parish school—is an important sign of Catholic education's renewed energy and entrepreneurialism. While largely autonomous parish-run schools will forever be an important part of K-12 Catholic schooling, we're now seeing useful variations on that theme. This experimentation is a positive sign.

Consortia are bringing independent parish schools together in creative ways. Networks are altogether reassigning authority over schools, innovating with curriculum, staffing, and more, and creating plans for growth. Chartering offers a way to preserve longstanding schools while moving explicitly religious education to before- and after-school programming. Blended and online models are personalizing learning and reducing costs. New curricular models are enabling schools to specialize their offerings to meet the varying interests of families.

> There is a strong appetite among parents for schools that provide classical liberal-arts education.

Catholic-school philanthropists eager to invest in promising new approaches now have countless options. There is ample room for innovation and change while preserving the core of Catholic education, as the examples in this chapter demonstrate. Nearly all of the initiatives highlighted here would benefit greatly from additional donor investments. Almost all are transportable to new cities and regions. Many of these fresh approaches could be combined in hybrid models. And there are options stretching far beyond the ones we have sketched here.

A donor might want to begin by deciding which local challenges he or she would most like to address. Enrollment losses? The need for new finance patterns? Competing with charter schools? Widening curricular options? Reaching more poor families? Attracting more middle-class families? There are opportunities in every direction. Then the donor can pick and choose from strategies being piloted across the nation. Happily, there is a growing range of tools that philanthropists can wield.

Your answer might be a nonprofit that takes over a string of struggling parish schools. It might be adding an online program of AP courses in one or more high schools. You may favor a values-infused charter school with wraparound Catholic services. Or something completely new and different could capture your imagination. More than at any time in the past, there is room for savvy social entrepreneurialism in Catholic education.

Investing in Talent

Prior to 1960, nearly all Catholic-school teachers and principals were members of religious communities—sisters, priests, or brothers. Today less than 3 percent of full-time Catholic-school staff are from an order. That transition has not been easy.

Half of the Catholic-school funders recently surveyed by The Philanthropy Roundtable identified a "lack of good school leaders" as among their three biggest concerns. "The way Catholic school leaders are recruited, selected, trained, and compensated is woefully inadequate," warns Stephanie Saroki de Garcia of Seton Education Partners. "If we're going to get serious," urges John Schoenig of ACE, "we have to attend to the school-level leadership issue."

"I have yet to see the supply of high-quality school leaders ever come close to the demand," the former superintendent of Paterson, New Jersey, Catholic schools, John Eriksen, told us. "This is in spite of a raft of Catholic school closures. Somehow, there still are never enough great leaders." Sister Rosemarie Nassif of the Conrad N. Hilton Foundation summarized succinctly that "principal leadership is the *driving force for success*. We need to seriously investigate ways to attract, develop, and retain high-performing Catholic school principals, including the provision of competitive compensation."

Calling all leaders

Catholic schools were spoiled by the essentially free work of generations of religious men and women—what was sometimes called "the living endowment." Lay educators require wages, benefits, and retirement plans that are at least reasonably consonant with district-run and charter schools. Today Catholic schools generally pay significantly lower salaries. The average base pay of a public-school teacher was $53,100 in 2012, compared to just $40,200 for private-school teachers of all sorts. Lower pay brings higher turnover. Of all private-school teachers today, 24 percent are in their first three years of teaching, compared to just 13 percent of public-school teachers.

Despite lower wages, religious and private schools do have advantages. Less than 5 percent of private-school teachers report that issues like student conflicts, disrespect for teachers, and children arriving unprepared to learn are "serious problems" at their schools. Public-school teachers report those things to be problems in their classrooms at about four times that rate.

When the Partnership for Inner-city Education took over a group of Catholic schools in New York City, the philanthropists driving the effort were able to hire Kathleen Porter-Magee as superintendent of the new network of schools. Prior to then, Porter-Magee was an executive at Achievement First, a high-performing charter chain, an adviser to the College Board, and an expert on Common Core curricula. Landing someone of Porter-Magee's caliber drew attention and praise for the Partnership.

It was the Partnership's energy and determination to make breakthroughs—and the exciting blank slate and big upside of Catholic schools—that attracted Porter-Magee. Her presence led in turn to other important hires. "It's very difficult to attract great talent into a broken business model," philanthropist Leo Linbeck points out. But where Catholic schools undertake creative management and open themselves to trying new things, their long history of pulling surprising accomplishments out of children can draw in impressive partners.

As Catholic schools make themselves a destination for high-potential talent (like today's top charter schools have), many good things will follow. Katie Everett of the Lynch Foundation urges the Catholic-school leaders she works with to organize their campuses, and then sell them to potential staff recruits, "as places where talented people want to build their careers." A question Russ Carson asks himself whenever he makes Catholic-school investments is "How do we create new structures and new processes so Catholic schools attract high performers who will make them successful?" It is a question others should ask as well.

It's not difficult work that scares away talented people, it's lack of vision and upside. The important work being done in urban Catholic schools is invigorating, life-enhancing activity, and if top teachers and leaders are given support and latitude to put their stamp on this activity, they can fuel the resurgence of an indispensable buttress to inner-city communities.

Leaders are made, not just born

Supporters must do much more to train the women and men who become teachers and principals in Catholic schools. Whether traditional preparation programs are up to the task, however, is very much in doubt. There is now a significant body of research questioning the link between traditional credentials from a teacher college and classroom effectiveness. Emphasizing paper credentials instead of passion and practical preparation in teachers is a problem at all schools today, not just Catholic institutions.

A particular reason to be cautious about conventional credentialing of teachers is that Catholic-school instruction has an extra dimension unrelated to what teacher colleges provide. Good Catholic schooling imparts not just academic skills but lessons in character, morals, and religious tradition, and this is closely linked to the surprising bang that Catholic schools get for their buck.

The work of Catholic-school teachers "is not only a job, a profession requiring specialized expertise," summarizes the National Catholic Educational Association, but "a ministry requiring courage and confidence." This element is important to parents, and to most donors. Steve Hoeppner describes the goal of the Schulze Family Foundation's Catholic-school support as not just "excellence in education" but also "expansion of access to moral and spiritual formation" among children.

With that in mind, what Catholic schools perhaps most need to create, copy, or fold themselves into today are the alternative paths to teaching that charter schools have created. These focus not on pedagogical theories but on very practical, empirically proven techniques, with a heavy emphasis on how to motivate children to put in extra effort and succeed, and a clear view of education as a moral mission. These alternative teacher-training paths have drawn into education thousands of bright, principled, passionate people who have never darkened the door of a teacher college.

It's not difficult work that scares away talented people. It's lack of vision and upside.

For instance, the nonprofit known as TNTP has quickly become one of the nation's most innovative and successful nontraditional teacher-preparation programs. It has prepared thousands of candidates to succeed in both conventional schools and charters. We asked its longtime leader Tim Daly whether lessons learned in trying to improve the training of public-school teachers could be brought to bear to help Catholic schools.

He noted that the initial impulse on the public-school side was to "work with entities that already produce teachers and hope to shape them so they produce the teachers needed." Unfortunately, "urban districts and charter-school organizations eventually realized that traditional teacher-prep programs would not turn out the quality or quantity of teachers they needed to elevate instruction substantially."

This same point was made by other experts we talked to. Saroki de Garcia expressed skepticism about conventional university-based programs: "I have seen funders invest gobs of money into starting teacher-development programs at their favorite Catholic universities. This rarely produces great leaders." Christine Healey of the Healey Education Foundation agreed, "A degree from an education school and certification alone does not determine a good leader or quality of leadership."

When charter-school leaders realized this, they decided to try something different: producing their own teachers. Though this can be challenging, when done right the result is "educators who are carefully selected and trained for the environments in which they'll work," as Daly puts it. See *Excellent Educators: A Wise Giver's Guide to Cultivating Great Teachers and Principals* for many examples of the alternative teacher training systems that are now turning out many of the instructors today's highest-quality schools seek most avidly.

Kate Walsh, president of the National Council on Teacher Quality, suggests Catholic-school donors shouldn't give up completely on conventional teacher programs. "Donors have an opportunity to put pressure on higher-ed institutions that aren't providing solid training to new teachers. (Donors should take a look at NCTQ's "Path to Teach" ratings, at PathtoTeach.org, to learn which programs are succeeding and which are falling short.) John Schoenig of Notre Dame's ACE urges donors to press Catholic colleges in particular to take hardheaded action to elevate teacher training. "Catholic higher education has to make substantial investments. They can't sit on the sidelines. They must play an integral role in the formation of our next generation of Catholic school leaders."

But it will probably be necessary to create some fresh, out-of-the-box training programs to put pressure on today's lumbering teacher-prep establishment. It was only when nontraditional paths into teaching like TNTP, Teach For America, the Relay Graduate School of Education, Match, and others exploded in popularity that the responsive teacher colleges began to institute some of the reforms that had made the new guys on the block more effective.

Whether donors choose to start something wholly new, partner with existing entrepreneurial efforts, or work with longstanding university-based programs, they really must put new emphasis in the future on the human element in Catholic schools. "We fund chefs, not kitchens. Nothing happens without good people," explains philanthropist Dan Peters. "Being a venture capitalist taught me to invest in people," agrees donor B. J. Cassin.

Following are programs that illustrate some of the initiatives under way to improve the pipelines that bring teaching talent and leadership skills into Catholic schools. Some are university-based, some are independent. Some focus on teachers, some on principals and network leaders. All are just beginning to address a need that is urgent.

Accelerate Institute

Formed in 2010 by the unification of three urban education programs, the Accelerate Institute focuses on training teachers and leaders to succeed

A note about professional development

Why does this chapter on talent focus primarily on identifying, recruiting, and training educators instead of developing those we already have? The unfortunate answer is because the research shows we simply don't know how to reliably improve a mature teacher's performance.

It's not because we haven't been trying. A new report by TNTP finds that school districts spend an average of $18,000 *per teacher per year* on professional development. Nevertheless, the researchers couldn't identify any strategies that produced significant performance gains. This sadly aligns with previous research, including studies done by the federal government's Institute of Education Sciences and National Center for Education Statistics.

There *are* wide variations in the effectiveness of teachers. And some educators *do* improve measurably in their early years. The profession has little idea, though, of how to identify teachers capable of improving, or of how to craft programs that will help them.

The past decade's most promising successes in improving the existing teacher force have been the Measures of Effective Teaching experiments funded by the Bill & Melinda Gates Foundation. These use test results, student surveys, and expert classroom observations to score how well teachers do at moving students further down the road of learning (regardless of where they start). When teachers are randomly assigned to different groups of students, their MET scores accurately predict which will be effective and which will flounder.

These measures are available for any school to take advantage of. And the logical next step is to begin to pay, fire, and hire teachers using scientifically developed measures of student progress— something that is being done with real success in Washington, D.C. and other cities. But this requires an unsentimental willingness to tell some teachers that their classroom results are substandard and that their gifts are not for leading children.

in tough, big-city neighborhoods. It works with district-run, charter, and faith-based schools throughout Chicago, and includes a specific track focused on Catholic schools. This "three-sector" approach is part of a "sector-neutral" movement catching on in many cities, and should be encouraged by donors keen to support what works, regardless of who is operating the school.

> It will be necessary to create some fresh training programs to put pressure on today's lumbering teacher-prep establishment.

It's important to ensure that three-sector programs actually respect the character and needs of Catholic schools. Their special characteristics can't be ignored or treated as a footnote. Accelerate has done a good job of incorporating a Catholic-school perspective into its teacher training. It was fortunate to have as its leader for a time Rob Birdsell—previously CEO of the hugely successful Cristo Rey Catholic schools, and currently leading the Drexel Fund that aims to propagate Catholic schools as a venture-capital firm would. (See Chapter 6 for details on the Drexel Fund.)

Alliance for Catholic Education
In 1994, two Notre Dame priests—Tim Scully and Sean McGraw—founded the ACE Teaching Fellows program. Often referred to as the "Catholic version of Teach For America," the fellowship places highly talented college graduates into Catholic schools in underserved communities for a two-year service experience. It combines professional training, spiritual development, and personal support (teachers live in community with other teachers). For years it has attracted some of the top graduating students from Notre Dame.

ACE teachers take master's-level coursework, ultimately earning a master of education degree from the University of Notre Dame, and they are eligible for teacher licensure in the state of Indiana. They live together in groups of four to seven peers during their fellowship placements, which helps fellows share burdens, successes, useful information, and emotional energy. The program immerses fellows in retreats, Masses, prayer services, and pastoral support.

The ACE program now places more than 170 highly competent college graduates in parochial schools across the country each year. Since its founding, it has trained more than 2,000 Catholic-school educators.

ACE also operates a program specifically created to train great principals. The Mary Ann Remick Leadership Program is a 25-month undertaking that leaves participants with both a Notre Dame master's degree in educational leadership and all the necessary coursework for a principal's credential from the state of Indiana. Remick Leaders complete a hands-on internship at a Catholic school, and take part in a helpful mentor workshop.

University Consortium for Catholic Education
In 1999 the University of Notre Dame hosted a meeting of Catholic universities running special teacher-education programs and those interested in starting such programs. These colleges began meeting twice annually, and in 2005 this informal rump group solidified into the University Consortium for Catholic Education. Today, the UCCE consists of 13 university-based alternative teacher certification programs that collectively place more than 400 teachers in Catholic schools each year.

All UCCE programs are modeled after ACE's successful teaching fellows. Fellows complete graduate coursework at their respective universities while spending two years serving as a full-time classroom teacher in a needy faith-based school. All participants deepen their faith and spiritual lives through dedicated retreats, prayer time, and worship, and all students live in community with other fellows during their two-year stint.

This pipeline of talent has become very important to Catholic-school principals, especially those in innovative networks. "We're trying to tap every elite Catholic college in the country" when hiring new teachers, reports Kathleen Porter-Magee of New York City's Partnership for Inner-city Education. "Next year, we'll have ACE teachers in our schools for the first time."

Lynch Leadership Academy
A gift from the foundation of legendary Fidelity Investments manager Peter Lynch and his wife, Carolyn, established the Lynch Leadership Academy in Boston in 2010. Offered through the Carroll School of Management at Boston College, it trains approximately 30 fellows each year. The program's application process is highly competitive. Fellows are drawn from the leadership of Catholic, charter, and district schools across Boston and its surrounding areas.

Alternative Programs for Training Catholic School Teachers

Program name	University
Alliance for Catholic Education (ACE)	University of Notre Dame
Alliance for Catholic Education at Saint Joseph's University	Saint Joseph's University
Gulf Region Academy for Catholic Educators	University of Saint Thomas
Lalanne	University of Dayton
Lasallian Association of New Catholic Educators	Christian Brothers University
Lutheran Educational Alliance with Parochial Schools	Valparaiso University
Loyola University Chicago Opportunities in Catholic Education	Loyola University
Magis Catholic Teacher Corps	Creighton University
Teachers Enlisted to Advance Catholic Heritage	Notre Dame of Maryland University
Pacific Alliance for Catholic Education	University of Portland
Providence Alliance for Catholic Teachers	Providence College
Partners in Los Angeles Catholic Education	Loyola Marymount University
Urban Catholic Teacher Corps	Boston College

Year launched	Regions served	Religious foundation
1993	15 states particularly in the South	Holy Cross
2010	Philadelphia and Camden, New Jersey	Jesuit
2008	Galveston-Houston	Basilian
1999	Cincinnati, Cleveland, Indianapolis, Lansing	Marianist
2003	Memphis	LaSallian
2001	Northern Illinois, northwest Indiana, and Cleveland	Lutheran
2005	Chicago	Jesuit
2001	Nebraska and South Dakota	Jesuit
2002	Baltimore Schools	Sisters of Notre Dame
1998	Portland, Seattle, Fairbanks, Salt Lake City, Sacramento, Spokane, and Yakima	Holy Cross
2001	New England	Dominican
2000	Los Angeles	Jesuit
1995	Boston	Jesuit

Katie Everett of the Lynch Foundation explains that *not* placing the academy in a traditional school of education was intentional, and important to success. "We put it in the business school," not just because "school leaders need to be good at budgeting, management, finance, and PR," but because this put some distance between the program and conventional ed-school orthodoxies.

The program's three-sector approach was also carefully formulated. "School leaders from charter, Catholic, and district schools have things in common. We've found that sharing good practices breaks down misconceptions about each sector. Peer-to-peer mentoring among professionals has a huge impact. Relationships among these different kinds of school leaders continue on. Eventually, people mainly care about good schools, instead of who is operating them."

For the 2014-2015 school year, the Lynch Academy selected 25 fellows from a pool of more than 170 applicants. They enter either an aspiring-principal track or the sitting-principal track. The program starts with a retreat and a two-week summer institute, then professional-development workshops and personal coaching are provided throughout the school year. Each fellow is paired with an instructor who offers 10 hours of individualized support each month and leads the fellow toward school goals.

Fellows accepted into the aspiring-principals program complete a yearlong residency in a Boston-area school in their sector (a Catholic school for Catholic leaders). Fellows work closely with that school's principal, who also serves as a mentor. Through this residency, aspiring principals gain experience leading instructor training, guiding team meetings, observing teachers and providing feedback, engaging with the community, and managing daily operations.

Lynch Academy graduates who have had their professional progress tracked demonstrate measurable improvement in staff management, problem solving, instructional leadership, and relationships. "We're hoping to expand the model to other districts in Massachusetts soon," says Everett. "And then to other parts of the country."

Fulcrum Foundation's pipeline for leaders

Two years ago the Fulcrum Foundation hired a mentor to support two Catholic-school leaders as they implemented a new blended-learning program. Each principal first worked with the mentor to develop a set of goals and priorities for the upcoming school year. Principals and expert then met weekly to discuss challenges and progress.

This assistance was offered because blended learning was new and uncharted territory for both leaders. Their mentor provided practical, hands-on support as they implemented the new technology and associated programs. That was very helpful in making this big transition successful at both schools.

Fulcrum Foundation director Anthony Holter ultimately realized, however, that "the biggest benefits came from the mentor building leadership skills in the principals, and working with school staff to set up leadership teams. We realized the program could address more root issues like school culture, capacity, expectations, discipline, and recruitment. We decided to capitalize on this and elevate leadership as a continuing place where we could be helpful in lots of ways for lots of Catholic schools. Our leadership academy is attempting to capture this."

The Fulcrum Foundation and the Seattle Archdiocese Office of Catholic Schools are in the early stages of developing a leadership pipeline to train existing and prospective Catholic-school principals. As currently conceptualized, this will have two main tracks: The first will offer candidates training sessions throughout the year with different departments in the archdiocese—budgeting, personnel, spiritual development, etc.—to improve performance in all these areas. The second part of the program will try to draw new talent into Catholic-school leadership. Current teachers, public-school principals, career-changers, and others will be offered preliminary instruction, then get an opportunity to apply to the Fulcrum Foundation for funding of graduate-program or certificate training that will qualify them to be a principal in a Catholic facility.

As of 2015, the Fulcrum Foundation is providing about 60 percent of the tuition so two fellows can attend the University of Notre Dame's Remick Leadership Program. Eventually, they aim to develop a list of "preferred providers"—schools with strong track records of educating high-quality Catholic school leaders—and let fellows choose their own programs. In exchange for tuition support, accepted candidates agree to serve in local Catholic schools for five years.

NYC Leadership Academy

The New York City Leadership Academy is a nonprofit that trains talented individuals to run high-quality schools for underserved students. Starting in 2003, the program was funded to address the dearth of highly effective principals in New York City's more than 1,200 public schools.

The program expanded beyond New York City, and since 2008 has worked with more than 40 clients in 26 states.

The organization primarily works with public-school districts, state departments of education, and universities. However it has helped the Consortium of Jewish Day Schools train principals for Jewish schools in California and New York City, and is currently partnering with the Commonweal Foundation to design a program specifically for faith-based schools. It could become a pipeline for Catholic schools in the future.

NYCLA offers a variety of services. It can teach schools or groups of schools how to launch their own leadership development programs. It runs three leadership programs itself: one for aspiring principals, one for current principals, and one for leaders on the district level. Each "emphasizes hands-on job-embedded learning, practical skills, and the ongoing self-reflection that enables educators to continue to build and refine their leadership practice."

PAVE

Governing boards are another place where the quality of Catholic-school leadership needs to be improved. Partners Advancing Values in Education is a Milwaukee-based nonprofit that assists religious and private schools in finding good candidates for school governing boards and then instructing them. PAVE has deep roots in the Catholic Church, having been launched in the 1980s initially to help Catholic schools raise money. From there it grew into a student-scholarship-granting organization. When the Wisconsin legislature created the state's voucher program in 1989, PAVE shifted its focus to offering information and services that strengthen Catholic, other religious and private, and charter schools. It has received strong funding from the Lynde and Harry Bradley Foundation and other Milwaukee donors.

"Our scholarships allowed kids to access the schools, but some of them were struggling, and faltering in quality as they served new populations," explains PAVE official Joan Feiereisen. "We went through a couple of phases as an organization trying to figure out how to help expand high-quality schools. We realized that many of the schools needed support with the business side of running a school, so we narrowed our focus to good governance," particularly recruiting and training board members.

"In the beginning, if the Catholic schools we were working with had a board at all, it was usually just a committee of parents who maybe advised the pastor or school principal on some issues. They weren't really making critical decisions for the schools. In some cases, schools didn't even have boards. School management was just an item on the church leadership's agenda. We needed to help schools realize the value of having a really quality governing board," explains Feiereisen.

PAVE helps schools find supporters with varied skills to serve. They look for talent and experience in areas like business management, law, marketing, finance, and education. All board members go through a "boot camp" which PAVE developed in conjunction with BoardSource, an organization that improves nonprofit boards of all sorts.

Boot camp instructs newly recruited board members on their roles and responsibilities, and provides needed background on the nuances of the Milwaukee and Wisconsin school contexts, including their nation-leading choice programs. The training consists of one eight-hour session followed by "deep-dives" into three or four particular subjects over a semester. These deep dives focus on topics like planning for succession at the head of the school, building better committees, mastering finance, fundraising tactics, and strategic planning. PAVE provides background resources on all these matters to all board members.

PAVE uses the same application and interview process when recruiting for religious schools, other private schools, or charters. Some candidates specify a particular type of school they wish to serve; most frequently PAVE matches individuals with schools based on their skills and school needs. "Recruitment has not been an issue at all," said Feiereisen. "We have lots of young professionals who are passionate about education and want to be change-agents in this city, as well as empty nesters who want to give back. We haven't had any trouble finding talented, interested people."

Over time PAVE has built trusting relationships with the schools it serves. It has been an invaluable influence on schools making the sometimes scary but important transition to a much stronger governing board. PAVE wants board members to be fully engaged with their school—especially the principal and pastor in a Catholic school. "There has to be trust there if this is going to work," explains Feiereisen.

One valuable side-effect of having a third-party nonprofit like PAVE serving a variety of schools citywide is the interconnections and spirit of camaraderie that often grow up among board members serving at different institutions. "Other board members can be really powerful allies and resources in this work," Feiereisen points out.

Schools That Can Milwaukee

Schools That Can Milwaukee brings together teachers and leaders from district, charter, and religious and private schools that participate in the region's school-choice programs. The organization is pursuing a goal of "20,000 by 2020"—creating 20,000 new, high-quality seats across all three sectors by that date. More than 175 educators from 38 schools in Milwaukee that enroll 14,000 students are currently active in STCM. The group is part of the national Schools That Can network, which also has affiliates in Chicago, Newark, and New York City.

The organization offers leadership coaching, teacher training, and peer-to-peer visits to high-quality schools. It brings to Milwaukee leaders of high-performing schools and innovative nonprofits from elsewhere, and works to transfer some of their successes to the locality. It recruits high-potential leaders for Milwaukee schools. And it has partnered with Alverno College and the Burke Foundation to create master's degree and licensing programs that hone principals to succeed in urban schooling.

Saint Remy Initiative

The Saint Remy Initiative is a partnership between the University of Dayton Center for Catholic Education and the Cincinnati Archdiocese Catholic School Office. Its purpose "is to provide Catholic-school principals and teachers with an opportunity to strengthen their knowledge and skills in the spiritual, academic, and managerial dimensions of their ministry." The program was inaugurated in 2007 with funding from the Joseph and Mary Keller Foundation.

Nine schools and 27 teachers and principals participated during the first year. By its eighth year, the program hosted 67 participants from 20 schools. It works on a three-year cycle, with each year focusing on a different pillar of Catholic-school leadership: spiritual, educational, and managerial.

"Most professional development for educators is a one-shot deal," states program founder Toni Moore. "But the most effective professional development focuses on the formation of the person, not just on acquiring skills. I wanted to create a program where personal and spiritual development is embedded throughout, where we are helping school leaders figure out all of who God has called them to be so they can really step into the calling in their schools."

Each year begins with a weeklong summer session covering personal spiritual growth, team-building, expert speakers, and time for school-level teams to develop a project that will strengthen the Catholic identify of their school. The summer session ends with a two-and-a-half-day tour of Ohio sites of historical significance to the Catholic faith. The identity-strengthening projects developed by school-level teams have included closer partnerships with the school's founding religious order, creating grade-level themes based on virtues (e.g., focusing third grade on justice, fourth on charity), and retreats to build understanding and closeness among school staff.

Participants also get four full days of professional development throughout the year. These daylong sessions include specific material on the subjects or grades that each person specializes in. Every year, specific books or topics are chosen for months-long study and discussion and then implementation of relevant content or skills into teaching.

Catholic Leadership Institute Project
CLIP, which grew out of the Saint Remy Initiative, trains Cincinnati-area principals using the management insights of Clay Mathile, founder of the Iams Company and an active philanthropist. After selling Iams for $2.3 billion, Mathile founded a nonprofit that provides entrepreneurial and free-enterprise education, and offers business owners training that will help them succeed and expand. A faithful Catholic, Mathile has included Catholic-school leaders among those eligible for management training. "We are trying to help Catholic-school leaders see that, in many ways, they are the CEOs of a business. They need to develop many of the same skills," explains Toni Moore.

About 25 Catholic-school principals participate in CLIP at any given time, progressing through the program in cohorts of six to eight individuals. They meet monthly in management-training sessions. And each principal is paired with a professional coach who helps implement the new practices back in their schools. "We want them to develop leadership skills for their schools, but also for the larger community of Catholic education," says Moore.

Talent must be the top priority
If backers of Catholic schooling are to turn today's propitious conditions into a full-fledged renaissance of the sector, they must focus on recruiting, developing, and retaining talent. No thriving system, no matter how smartly built, can be made people-proof. Governance change, school-choice advocacy, building consortia and networks, providing

back-office services—these things are all important and valuable places for philanthropists to contribute. "You could do everything else right, but terrible leadership will close a school," warns donor Christine Healey.

Good strategies will only go as far as the people leading them. The traditional pipelines of human capital that allowed Catholic schools to mushroom—dedicated sisters and parish priests—completely evaporated a generation ago. New leaders with new competencies are desperately needed.

Donors eager to reinforce Catholic schools should recall NHL-great Wayne Gretzky's famous line about his uncanny ability to consistently be several steps ahead of his opponents: "I skate to where the puck is going to be, not where it has been." Philanthropists should build talent for tomorrow's system of Catholic education, not yesterday's.

> No thriving system, no matter how smartly built, can be made people-proof. If you have weak leaders, even donor-kissed schools will tank.

Catholic schooling in the future will be marked by more independent, non-parish schools, more networks, more specialized academic programs, more advocacy for improved public policies, and other changes. The sector needs to prepare accordingly. "These schools are 2-plus-million-dollar operations. You can't say they're not businesses," states longtime Catholic-school donor John Stollenwerk. "But pastors don't have training in finance or business, much less fundraising. Bishops don't either. We need to do what businesses do, what universities and hospitals do. We have to change, or else these schools are going to fold."

What kinds of talent will be needed, what information and skills must individuals possess, in order for Catholic schools to thrive in the future? Existing programs need to be re-positioned in those directions. And new organizations are unquestionably needed. In the great hunt to come for the requisite talent, donors will be essential.

Advocacy and Policy Change

For donors interested in funding public education and policy advocacy in support of Catholic schools, two anecdotes may be instructive.

One: In Wichita, Kansas, all Catholic primary and secondary schools have been tuition-free since 2002. How did that happen? Local pastor Thomas McGread challenged his flock to donate 5 percent of their incomes so all children in the parish could attend the elementary school for free. When his congregation rose to the challenge, he asked them to donate 8 percent so the parish could pay the Catholic high-school tuition of any local child. Again, the parishioners stepped up. Today, under the leadership of Bishop Michael Jackels, Catholic schooling in Wichita continues to grow—enrollment now stands at its highest level since 1967.

Two: In March 2015 more than 100 lay Catholic leaders, including donors like former American Express president Alfred Kelly and former PricewaterhouseCoopers CEO Samuel Di Piazza, gathered with Cardinal Timothy Dolan to discuss a new political action committee aimed at preserving New York's Catholic schools. The product of those conversations, "Catholics Count," has already raised $3 million and has a goal of raising $10 million over the next four years to help it compete meaningfully in the state's capital. "Finally the Catholic Church will have a voice in Albany commensurate with our numbers and with the contributions our church makes to our state and to our communities," says donor Robert Flanigan.

The first story shows that members of the wider public can be mobilized to support Catholic schools if someone will start things with a simple ask. It just takes leadership to energize the latent support for Catholic education. The second tale demonstrates that impressive things can happen when Church leaders, philanthropists, and other advocates for Catholic education combine forces behind a focused goal.

Keep those two examples in mind as you read this chapter on what donors can do to turn opinion and public policy in helpful directions. Catholic-school backers should be energetic in bringing the benefits of their institutions to the attention of fellow citizens. And they should join in cooperative efforts to nudge law and policy in constructive directions.

Communicating with the general public

Much of this chapter will deal with efforts to make public policies more friendly to Catholic education. But it's worth noting that simply making the general public more aware of Catholic schools is also important work. As parents, neighbors, voters, and citizens, families need to know about Catholic schools and their many benefits to students and surrounding communities.

Several organizations engage methodically in this activity. The National Catholic Educational Association has been explaining Catholic schools to Americans for a century. The United States Conference of Catholic Bishops sometimes engages on K-12 education.

The Council for American Private Education supports Catholic as well as other non-government schools by serving as a unified voice on issues important to private education. It advocates, informs private-school leaders about relevant developments, and sponsors gatherings. The National Association of Independent Schools also produces research, provides guidance on governance and other operational issues, and offers professional development opportunities for Catholic and other private schools.

There are also lots of state and local groups supporting Catholic schooling. Donors eager to build wider understanding and support for Catholic schools need not start from scratch. In many cases they can reinforce organizations with networks and infrastructure already in place.

Promoting changes in public policy

A reliable stream of operational funding is essential to all organizations. Because Catholic schools often serve low-income families, they have to keep tuition far below what other private schools charge. Yet they are aiding American society, both by turning underprivileged kids into graduates and solid citizens at unusually high rates, and by saving taxpayers the much higher cost of educating those children in public schools. Accordingly a highly important, and easily justified, component of Catholic-school advocacy is the creation, expansion, and defense of laws that allow parents to have their choices of accredited private or religious schools for their children matched with some sort of public funding. The Hilton Foundation is now putting more effort into expanding public funding of choice programs, and helping schools participate. "We initially focused our grantmaking in Los Angeles," reports Sister Rosemarie Nassif. Then the foundation shifted toward "private-school choice advocacy and implementation. We want to ensure Catholic schools take advantage of such programs." "The highest-leverage strategy for saving inner-city Catholic schools is through school choice," suggests entrepreneur and donor Leo Linbeck. "Small amounts of money invested to get states to create or increase tax credits and vouchers can go a long way."

These programs enable low-income and working-class families to give their children much improved futures. They also make it likelier that Catholic schools will exist in the future for other families to take advantage of. Even the fragmentary tax credit and voucher programs that currently exist have been very helpful in generating funds and stabilizing enrollments at Catholic schools.

A report on this question by the American Catholic bishops urges that:

> We need to intensify our efforts in advocating just and equitable treatment of our students and teachers in federal and state-funded educational programs.... Advocacy is not just the responsibility of parents and teachers, but of all members of the Catholic community. As the primary educators of their children, parents should have the right to choose the school best suited for them. The entire Catholic community should be encouraged to advocate for parental school choice and personal and corporate tax credits, which will help parents to fulfill their responsibility.

Entanglements with government have their downside. Joe Womac of the Specialty Family Foundation warns schools against thinking that choice reimbursements will relieve them of the need to pay close attention to internal operations, cost control, enrollment management, and fundraising. Most public voucher and tax-credit measures today cover only a small fraction of total expenses per pupil. Ed Kirby, former executive at the Walton Family Foundation, encourages schools to run themselves in ways that would keep them stable even if there was no public funding. Then the public reimbursements, if they materialize, offer opportunities to grow and become more excellent.

Types of school-choice programs

The first modern school-choice payments were enacted in Wisconsin in 1989. Today, 57 different school-choice funding programs exist in 29 states. Vouchers and tax credits are the commonest offerings.

Providing vouchers to parents allows education dollars to "follow the child" to the school his family considers best for him. As of 2015, 24 of the 57 state choice programs were vouchers. The tax-credit approach recognizes nonprofits that exist to provide scholarships to low-income students so they can attend religious or private schools, and allows tax credits for individuals or businesses that donate money to these nonprofits. As of 2015, 20 of the 57 choice programs were tax-credit scholarship programs. Some states also allow parents to save up K-12 school tuition in education savings accounts that somewhat reduce the family's tax exposure. A few states provide individual tax credits for tuition payments as partial help so parents can access religious and private schools.

Programs vary in the restrictions they place on student eligibility. Twenty-three programs are means-tested to keep them focused on low-income families. Eight programs are limited to children who are attending the state's worst public schools. Fourteen programs are aimed at students with special needs.

The total number of students with access to non-public school-choice assistance has grown rapidly. In 2000, just 29,000 students attended a religious or private school with public support. In 2014-15 nearly 354,000 did. This expansion is likely to extend further, perhaps into states like New York in the near future. At the moment, though, six states—Florida, Arizona, Pennsylvania, Indiana, Ohio, and Wisconsin—account for nearly nine out of ten of the students who have school-choice benefits.

Effects of programs

The effects on students of attending a private school through a voucher or tax-credit program have been documented in many studies. As early as 1998, research on the Milwaukee Parental Choice Program found that students who enrolled in a participating private school using a voucher had faster math gains than identical students who applied for, but did not receive, a voucher. A 2011 report by the Friedman Foundation for Educational Choice conglomerated ten voucher studies and found that six showed positive results for all types of students, three found positive results on some student groups, and only one found no positive results. A randomized experimental study of the Washington, D.C., voucher program found that the program had a large positive impact on the high school graduation rates of participating students.

In 2000, just 29,000 students attended a religious or private school with public support. In 2014-2015 nearly 354,000 did.

In addition to their value to students, research has found that voucher programs have positive competitive effects on educational systems as well. In Louisiana, the voucher program positively influenced the performance of the lowest-rated public schools. In Indiana, the voucher program improved public schools' reading scores. Research on Ohio's EdChoice program found that the competitive effects created by vouchers had a positive impact on the public elementary and middle schools whose families were eligible for vouchers.

There are also benefits in terms of parental satisfaction. A 2002 study found that voucher families reported higher levels of satisfaction on 16 variables, including "academic program," "teacher skills," "school discipline," "safety," and "teacher-parent relations." Other research found that parents who used a voucher were 25 percentage points more likely to rate their school as "A" or "B."

Limits on programs

School-choice programs often have restrictions that limit families' access. One study sorted these restrictions into three categories:

- Student restrictions that exclude children based on demographic characteristics or via a cap on the total size of the program
- Purchasing-power restrictions that limit the amount of money a program will provide to a family
- School restrictions that reduce the range of schools from which families can select

A sample of 21 choice programs were studied using this framework. The highest rated (Florida's McKay Voucher Program) earned an A-minus. Fourteen programs were scored between B and B-plus. Six earned a C or lower. Most of today's school-choice programs are very partial and thin, and the various limits on eligibility end up excluding most families. So while the momentum in this area is promising, there is enormous room for expansion and improvement.

Cumbersome program demands on schools can also lead many of them to decline to participate. The red tape in some of today's school-choice programs includes banning student admissions criteria, requiring certain curricula, insisting students are offered chances to opt out of religious activities, tuition controls, test requirements, teacher and administrator credentialing, stipulations on instructional hours, open-enrollment requirements, and heavy paperwork for each participating student. A quarter or more of all schools opt not to accept vouchers when they come with these kinds of strings, particularly if the payments are small to begin with.

One study of schools that decided not to participate in state school-choice programs found that the reform most likely to change their mind would be to expand eligibility to all families (38 percent of non-participating schools said that would alter their decision). Raising voucher amounts was the next strongest influencer.

Families using Catholic schools typically take advantage of choice programs, where they exist, at rates over 70 percent. This reflects the Catholic-school mission of particularly serving the poor. Catholic schools are therefore disproportionately affected when onerous regulations are woven into choice programs. Donors should be mindful of this downside as they advocate for particular details in choice programs.

Accountability in school-choice programs

In contrast to the intrusive regulations that weaken some school-choice programs, many of the largest programs include useful measures that hold schools accountable for performance results. Requiring private schools to administer standardized tests to participating students in order to ensure that the schools are helping kids learn is an example. In Louisiana, all private schools receive a performance rating based on these test results, and schools with persistently low performance are removed from the program. In Indiana, all religious and private schools are evaluated under the same A-F rating system used for public schools, and private schools with persistently low ratings can be suspended from the choice program. In Milwaukee, participating choice schools must publicly report the test scores of their voucher students.

These accountability measures are designed to ensure that funds are well spent and that families have access to *high-quality* choices. The Thomas Fordham Institute argues that good accountability measures on private school-choice programs may be beneficial for at least six reasons:

- They create incentives for schools to boost student achievement
- They give parents access to crucial information they need to judge schools
- They won't scare away reputable schools
- They work proportionately—schools that accept more voucher students and thus rely more heavily on state funding are held to higher levels of accountability
- They make fair comparisons of schools easier
- They are the foundation for a "grand bargain" that needs to be extended much further across our educational sector—accountability and good results in exchange for solid financial support

Hard evidence exists that implementing accountability standards does indeed increase student performance. For instance, when new legislation required schools participating in the Milwaukee choice program to annually test all voucher students in grades 3-8 and grade 10 using the statewide knowledge exams, studies showed a significant positive impact on the achievement of all subgroups. Gains were strongest for students with higher levels of initial ability.

Not everything of value produced by schools can be easily measured. Catholic schools in particular often distinguish themselves less in test scores than in things like high graduation rates, high levels of college persistence and success by their alumni, high levels of service and good citizenship among their students, and so forth. Catholic schools put heavy emphasis on character traits and skills that may not yield higher end-of-year test scores, though they have great life value.

So donors will want to avoid a sole fixation on test scores. Yet they should not get swept into the forswearing of annual tests and other hard measures of performance—an increasingly trendy and ideological position that only makes it easier for mediocre or incompetent educators to coast, and that shifts the conversation about schooling to just pouring in more inputs (money) rather than pursuing better outcomes. The hard glare of performance tests makes the educational establishment sweaty, but is ultimately vital to helping children. Donors needn't get drawn deeply into the testing debate, but they must understand the basic contours—because the topic is important and colors many other elements of today's school-reform tussle.

Active state and national advocacy
Some states have single-purpose advocacy organizations whose reason for being is to advance parental options in schooling. School Choice Ohio would be an example. There are also a number of excellent education-advocacy organizations that operate at the national level while also sponsoring state-level affiliates or state-level activities. These include 50CAN, Students First, Stand for Children, the Black Alliance for Educational Options, and others. Donors can support useful advocacy by working through such organizations. They will need to find out which have operations in their states, which have recently shown the ability to be successful, and which are fully committed to Catholic schools.

A donor should also take the time to understand her state's particular political context and history with school-choice legislation and proposals. These will help determine the best strategies. Historically, notes Tom Carroll, president of the Coalition for Opportunity in Education, "school-choice proposals have been more successful below the Mason-Dixon line and in right-to-work states. Yet in states with powerful teacher unions, successes have occurred under strong Republican governors like Mitch Daniels, Tommy Thompson, or Tom Ridge." With school choice now spreading nationwide, Carroll

> Donors should support annual tests and other hard measures of performance.

believes philanthropists can help execute successful campaigns even in previously hostile locations. "Current work in New York and Illinois shows that Democratic constituencies can be pulled together around school choice. It is not easy work, and the odds are steep. But there's great potential, given the right approach."

Donors must be prepared for a long haul. The campaign by Indiana school-choice advocates, for instance, took eight years before it produced their landmark school-voucher program. Then more time was required to plan a good roll out. School choice is important, and it requires stamina.

American Federation for Children

The American Federation for Children Growth Fund is a leader across the nation in organizing and providing information on behalf of school choice that includes private and religious schools. As successor to the Alliance for School Choice, which served as the main umbrella organization for a decade, the AFC Growth Fund publishes data on school choice, basic information on programs by state, model legislation, and the annual *School Choice Yearbook*, which tracks school information and the latest trends in advocacy across the country.

The Growth Fund also invests in states with potential for enacting or expanding school-choice programs. It develops state leaders, communicates with policymakers about the importance of school choice, supports parent advocacy, and helps implement choice programs. As a 501(c)(3) it does not partake in lobbying or direct political work.

Its sister organization the American Federation for Children is a 501(c)(4) organization that is equipped to lobby and advocate with officeholders. A third partner, the American Federation for Children Action Fund, is a 527 political-action committee that supports candidates for political office who have been helpful to the cause of school choice. School reformers in many places have found this tripartite structure of information and local support, lobbying, and political backup for allies to be the most effective way to support constructive change.

The American Federation for Children has partner organizations in 24 states. These included groups like the Alabama Policy Institute, the Louisiana Federation for Children, Excellent Education for Everyone in New Jersey, and the REACH Foundation in Pennsylvania. Donors interested in choice advocacy should investigate whether their priority states have such partner organizations.

Donor Betsy DeVos, who chairs the boards of both the AFC and the AFC Growth Fund, points out that "successful advocacy requires coordinating a lot of moving parts: identifying potential legislators, educating them about the issue, getting them elected, helping them craft and pass legislation, and helping with implementation once laws are passed to ensure that programs work for children." Donors should not underestimate the implementation task. It may be less glamorous than passing legislation, but it's important.

Choice legislation only works if, for example, there are high-quality private schools from which to choose, and parents have good information on the available options, and the government bodies charged with administration are helpful. There are always early-stage hiccups to address. Allies need to be rallied to support parents and programs. Once a governor's signature is affixed to a law, donors should help make sure it is executed so as to succeed.

Friedman Foundation for Educational Choice

Nobel laureate Milton Friedman and his economist wife, Rose Friedman, established the Friedman Foundation for Educational Choice in 1996. It is a leading advocate for universal school choice today. The foundation provides in-depth research reports—including gold-standard national and state studies of choice programs, plus polling data. Its major publications include the "ABCs of School Choice," a national public-opinion survey on education, state-level polls on school choice, and pithy white papers on key topics within school choice.

The foundation partners with local nonprofits, schools, businesses, parents, and community members to help them advocate for school choice. It sponsors events and seminars. It helps design programs, supports testimony before state legislatures, and provides grants for state activities. Like the American Federation for Children, the Friedman Foundation works across the policy life cycle—measuring public opinion on school choice, striving to improve it, developing policy, supporting local partners in advocating for change, and following up on implementation issues.

Investing in data collection and research

As existing school-choice programs expand and new ones are created, some donors might want to concentrate on promoting more *high-quality* choices. Supporting the collection and reporting of student performance data can help separate poor and mediocre schools from those that advance their students. Collecting performance data can also demonstrate the successes of school choice, thereby easing advocacy for new and expanded programs.

Donors might partner with think tanks, universities, or state departments of education to fund rigorous evaluations. National organizations like the Thomas Fordham Institute, the Center for Education Reform, the CATO Institute, and the American Enterprise Institute are deeply

> Collecting performance data can demonstrate the successes of school choice, easing advocacy for new and expanded programs.

involved in this kind of work. So too are state-level think tanks like School Choice Indiana and StudentsFirst PA. Both the Center for Education Reform and the State Policy Network maintain databases of state-based think tanks that are advocating for market-oriented education policies including school choice.

Regardless of how a donor chooses to fund advocacy efforts, it is important to bear in mind that most advocacy will be state-specific. Givers will be most effective if they understand the history of their state programs, their student eligibility rules, what caps they have on the number of students or scholarships, which schools are eligible, the programs' performance data, and more. In states where programs do not yet exist, donors should learn about previous and/or ongoing efforts to enact school choice.

The type and quality of choice program matters, so donors should make sure policies are drafted with the most recent lessons and successes and pitfalls of other programs in mind. And experience has taught that events during the implementation phase can threaten school choice even after legislative success has been achieved. Beware of low-performing private schools that produce poor results, letting public funds get mismanaged by schools, families failing to participate due to lack of information or transportation gaps, and so forth. Familiarity with the record in other places can prevent these sorts of unnecessary and potentially damaging mishaps.

Investing in marketing

Donors can be enormously helpful to Catholic schools by helping them market themselves to families. As Faith in the Future's Casey Carter said, "How do you get more revenue? Get more students in the school. How do you do that? Market and sell your product for the first time. But you can't sell the same old product. You need to compete on both quality and price, and not just your reputation from the past."

For schools under financial stress, growing your way to balanced books is much preferable to cutting your way to balance. Yet some schools lose or actually turn away potential students because they fail to market themselves and resist things like marginal tuition discounts to bring in additional students.

To help with this, the Specialty Family Foundation in Los Angeles has provided schools with large three-year grants so they could bring in expert marketing help. That allowed them to get serious about outreach, advertising, and development, according to Specialty's Joe Womac. Too often, he says, Catholic educators "talk about enrollment like they talk about the weather—it's up one day, down the next, and out of their control. They don't see themselves as variables at all."

In many locations, Catholic schools are part of a competitive schools marketplace, yet many families know little about what they really offer. The sector often hasn't differentiated itself with any specificity. "Part of the reason Catholic schools started to fail is because they didn't figure out and explain their unique benefits," argues Katie Everett of the Lynch Foundation.

School leaders need to be encouraged to market themselves not just to parents, but to supporters as well. Parishioners, leaders of the community where the school is located, and potential donors also need to see the value of Catholic schooling. Getting surrounding stakeholders excited about the high mission of these schools, as the Wichita leaders did, as described in the beginning of this chapter, is the best basis for fundraising, suggests donor Christine Healey.

Donors who are involved in education reform broadly can help make sure that when school districts, and cities, and states are considering new policies of educational accountability, teacher effectiveness, classroom technology support, school busing, charter schooling, and so forth, Catholic schools are included in the discussion. As one philanthropist put it at a recent meeting of The Philanthropy Roundtable, "Catholic schools struggle to represent themselves and communicate their value within today's school reform movement. The broader movement tends to focus on creating new seats. But Catholic schools already *have* seats—they just haven't figured out yet how to make these seats and their schools a viable part of the education-reform conversation."

Finding your place

Donors providing funding to Catholic education should recognize that advocacy, marketing, and policy change are ways to multiply and sustain their influence. Philanthropists who are prepared to add this crucial work to their direct assistance to students and schools should begin by thinking through three questions.

First, *what kind of public programs do I want to support?* As school-choice legislation has proliferated, it has also diversified. There are vouchers, tax-credits, education savings accounts, and more. Which schools benefit, what students are eligible, how mechanisms of distribution and accountability work—these things all vary. Donors need to set priorities before their advocacy begins.

Second, *where do I want to engage?* A donor might focus on producing data and research that prove success. Or on wooing policymakers and helping them develop constructive rules for school-choice programs. Or he or she might pay for a public-relations campaign aimed at legislators, families, community leaders, or potential fellow donors. An individual donor might make personal contributions to political campaigns and engage with candidates and elections as a supplement to charitable efforts. In a state that is already over the political hump and is now struggling to implement public spending in ways that really help children and families, a donor might decide to work on measures that improve the supply or quality of schools, the felicity of government administration of the funding, or the accountability of teachers and leaders in the recipient schools.

A third question is, *with whom should I partner?* Philanthropists ought to avoid reinventing the wheel to the extent possible. Yet they should be picky suitors. Not all organizations and campaigns are created equal. Depending on your goals, it could make sense to work with a particular church leader, with a Catholic-school support organization, with a state advocacy group, or with a major national nonprofit. There are options aplenty.

Fundamental Change Via a Citywide Approach

This guidebook has identified lots of discrete initiatives that could be launched in support of Catholic schooling. Some donors might want to set their sights even higher, though, and aim for systemic change that would put Catholic schools on more solid footing for the long haul. Specifically, some ambitious philanthropist could set out to create a "system of schools" in his or her home city that goes beyond the conventional government-run school district to include a wide array of academies—including

Catholic schools—while offering families opportunities to choose among all of these schools without prejudice as to school type, and with equivalent economic support.

The school reform that would be most meaningful today would be to stop assigning children to schools and instead to let parents decide which programs are best suited for each of their children. This approach has been building momentum for decades. Nobel-winning economist Milton Friedman recommended universal vouchers 50 years ago. John Chubb and Terry Moe's seminal 1990 book *Politics, Markets, and America's Schools* put empirical evidence behind that argument. Writers like Paul Hill and Ted Kolderie have mulled ways of opening up a diverse supply of school options. Andy Smarick's 2012 book *The Urban School System of the Future* brings many of these ideas together in a "three-sector approach" where public authorities would apply the same even-handed standards to conventional schools, charter schools, and private or religious schools, and let funding follow children to whichever institution fit them best.

Given the events of the past two decades this is no longer a daydream. Three million students (in some cities, a majority) now attend charter schools. We're approaching 60 private-school choice programs operating in more than 20 states. Several states have adopted "education savings accounts" and measures that enable students to steer portions of state education aid to institutions they attend. In Boston and Philadelphia, metropolitan compacts have been established that put Catholic and other religious schools on equal footing with conventional schools in official systems providing parents with school information and enrollment forms for their children.

Such revolutionary openings-up of our formerly closed public-school systems are almost certainly going to continue. We recommend that Catholic-school philanthropists not only focus on the schools and children where learning is taking place *today*, but also engage in the national effort to re-imagine future urban schooling on a fair three-sector basis. Big ideas are percolating and big changes may be within reach.

Catholic-school donors can and should contribute to this war of ideas. Donor Leo Linbeck poses the central question: "Do you want to take the environment as given, or shape it?" Kathy Almazol, superintendent of Catholic schools in San Jose urges that "We need more people who have the vision for change. Then we can start assembling people with the work ethic, skills, and capacity to bring it to pass." Christine Healey of the Healey Family Foundation argues that Catholic schools, many of which have slack capacity that could be put to use relatively quickly, need to be folded into the wider school-reform coalition like charter schools have been over the last decade or so.

"Too often, philanthropists only want to invest in their own backyards," warns Stephanie Saroki de Garcia. "They know their communities and needs, and they want to see their impact. But Catholic education won't advance unless philanthropists begin to think much more broadly, funding leaders and ideas that have the potential to show what's possible, even if it's not in their own backyards. The charter sector benefited greatly from a dozen or so funders getting together regularly to talk about strategic needs nationally in the sector. The dramatic education gains in New Orleans happened because of a coalescing of national funders who saw an opportunity to demonstrate change, and invested in it, despite not having roots in the city. Their successes in New Orleans have had a national ripple effect. Catholic-education funders can learn from this smart strategy."

> The school reform that would be most meaningful today would be to stop assigning children to schools, and instead let parents choose.

Whenever local education decisions are made, donors should look for every opportunity to have their region's Catholic schools included at the table. Catholic schools can and should be seen as an integral part of a city's portfolio of schools, right alongside charter, district-run, and other private schools. This might not come naturally to some Catholic-school leaders—who at times see the charter sector as the opponent not an ally. But as Katie Everett of the Lynch Foundation argues, "Catholic schools need to stop vilifying charters." They should recognize the places they can make common cause on behalf of real education choice, and they should compete and engage in order to improve their own product.

Bear in mind how much the nation's thinking about schooling has changed in the past 25 years. In 1990 and before, there was a clear and very wide gulf between public and private schooling. On the public side, the school district was the lone operator of all government-funded schools.

To "support" public education typically meant aligning yourself with that monopoly provider and opposing all other means of delivering education.

Then the charter-school movement showed that a range of non-government entities can run public schools—that public education doesn't require a sole government provider. About the same time, tax credits, vouchers, education savings accounts, and other school-choice mechanisms were proliferating, offering more and more students real options. The public is growing used to the idea that "private" schools also serve the public good, and shouldn't be denied education dollars. The pre-1990 sense of what is "public" in schooling has been rendered anachronistic. These changes demand fresh thinking about the right approach to citywide reform efforts, and donors can lead the charge.

Shifting to quality and growth

What some call "sector agnosticism" or "sector neutrality"—funding all students in high-quality schools without worrying about who runs those schools—would put the focus of education reform on school performance and family choice rather than on glacial efforts to re-engineer daily operations within government-run schools that continue to dominate public funding. Sector neutrality opens up true competition; it creates a way for new school models to develop, grow, and thrive; it puts the users of schools in the driver's seat and thus fuels creativity and innovation to satisfy parents and students.

The other thing a sector-neutral approach does is to make the high-quality school king. Once we have fair, transparent systems for measuring a school's performance without fussing over who is operating it, donors can jump in to expand or replicate the most effective institutions. Donors would, in the words of Adam Hawf, one of the educators who helped turn around Louisiana schools after Hurricane Katrina, be able "to take a more muscular approach to investing in a high-quality supply of schools." In any new regime that is fair to all schools that perform well, Hawf believes Catholic schools will have a substantial role to play. He urges philanthropists to help leaders of today's most excellent Catholic schools expand their facilities and launch new campuses.

This kind of growth mindset may not come naturally to many traditional Catholic-school leaders, after having spent recent decades back on their heels. For years, "expansion" simply meant filling the empty seats in existing schools. In the next phase of Catholic schooling it will mean finding the best schools and creating more of them.

To help the sector prepare for this shift, donors might think about investing in two foundation-laying strategies. First, nudge Catholic-school leaders toward this new approach. Base spending decisions upon it. For example, if your city has an academically struggling school with 100 empty seats and an academically superior school that is at capacity, you should prioritize the latter for growth.

Second, donors need to start grooming the next generation of Catholic-school leaders by looking for individuals with a streak of social entrepreneurialism, a growth mentality, and an interest in playing a part in a citywide "system of schools." Future superintendents and principals must be able to look beyond their own parking lot and envision themselves within the exciting new metropolitan approaches to school reform that are beginning to emerge.

The Drexel Fund, the new philanthropic pool that will provide venture capital to expand the supply of Catholic schools, is a systematic way of investing in quality. The fund is the creation of Rob Birdsell, former CEO of the Cristo Rey Network and the Accelerate Institute; B. J. Cassin, an investor and major Catholic-schools philanthropist; and John Eriksen, former superintendent of Catholic schools in Paterson, New Jersey. Officially opened in 2015, the Drexel Fund will initially target six states with solid public programs that support private schools (e.g. vouchers, tax credits): Florida, Arizona, Ohio, Louisiana, Wisconsin, and Indiana. Its first seed investments went out in fall 2015.

The Drexel Fund is modeled after two well-known philanthropic funds that have been important in expanding the supply of excellent charter schools: the Charter School Growth Fund and the NewSchools Venture Fund. "We are very much of the mindset that if it's great, the school should be serving more kids," explained Rob Birdsell. "If someone has a great school, why should their growth be limited? Let's get creative. They need funding to expand and serve more students and families."

The Drexel Fund, which was named in honor of Saint Katharine Drexel, a Catholic nun who founded schools for Native- and African-American students in the early 1900s, plans to ultimately raise $85 million and invest that to create 50,000 new seats in high-quality schools that serve low- and middle-income families. Over the next decade the fund hopes to aggressively expand six to eight successful school networks, create 125 altogether new schools, and develop 40 new entrepreneurs to work in private schools.

Voluntary Catholic-school performance contracts?

One of the most important innovations of charter schooling is the performance contract. A charter-school operator gets the chance to run a publicly funded school in exchange for signing a performance contract with a responsible official entity. That external accountability body is typically known as an "authorizer" or "sponsor." Its board gives the school huge latitude on how it organizes and manages itself, but monitors the charter school's progress toward its performance targets, and renews or withdraws authorization depending on how well the school ultimately serves students.

There are several important benefits to this system. It clarifies the expectations for a school. It allows leaders wide operational autonomy—since everyone has agreed on what measurable outcomes are expected, guardians of the public purse feel comfortable in freeing up educators to decide on inputs. It gives parents objective indicators of the school's performance. It gives the government confidence that public funding will be put to good use. Performance contracts were the magic element that convinced authorities to let go of government management as a *sine qua non* of public schooling.

Charter schools are required to have performance contracts. The same benefits could be realized by religious and private schools, however, if they voluntarily signed performance contracts. It would be an extraordinarily useful experiment for donors to pilot a kind of authorizer/sponsor system for Catholic schools.

This might work in two ways. A donor could fund a relationship between an existing charter-school authorizer with a good track record and a set of Catholic schools in its geographic region. The authorizer would use its normal processes to develop a performance agreement with each participating Catholic school. The schools would be able to maintain all aspects of their Catholic identity, but they would be assessed for academic achievement in the same way as charter schools, and results would be publicized in the same way. No public money would change hands, and the authorizer wouldn't be able to close a Catholic school for underperformance, but the experiment would encourage excellent performance, show how the school stacks up against similar institutions, provide a template showing what would happen if Catholic schools were treated like charters, and cement the deepening public understanding that all schools serving children well operate in the public interest, no matter who manages them.

An alternative approach would be to create a new, independent city-specific Catholic-school accountability body. Since most cities now have multiple Catholic school operators (some run by parishes, others by the diocese, others by networks, some independent), a single external entity could be funded by donors to enter into performance agreements with each. The contracts could be individualized to allow for demographic and other school-level differences. But they'd also share some common elements with each other and with local charter-school accountability expectations, so comparisons would be possible.

An authorizer system like this would focus everyone's attention on specific goals, provide invaluable information to families and donors, and identify schools' areas of strength and weakness. It would also help make the case that a city's Catholic schools are being held accountable and therefore should be eligible for funding through a public program like vouchers. Through a "prove your performance" pilot program, a savvy donor might be able to pull Catholic schools onto the trajectory that has made charters so successful over the past decade.

"The Catholic Church does so many things and has so many responsibilities that running, much less replicating, great schools can get lost or de-prioritized," observes Drexel co-founder John Eriksen. Citing the charter sector he notes that "the people who have been successful in starting and expanding excellent schools have focused on that one task." Drexel will fill that role.

Cassin, who donated $1 million in seed money and recruited several other founding donors, explains his motivation. "There are a lot of interesting new models in faith-based and especially Catholic schools, but we don't have a platform to replicate the most successful ones. That's where the idea of Drexel came from."

Practical citywide strategies

In addition to supporting the growth and replication of Catholic schools through venture-capital organizations like the Drexel Fund, donors can be directly involved in replicating high-performing Catholic schools in their own cities. Philanthropic funding should be used to transfer to the Catholic-school world three successful strategies that have emerged in the charter sector: school incubators, growth accelerators, and harbormasters.

Incubators have been helpful to charter advocates in meeting the need for more high-quality schools. They start by recruiting, training, and evaluating promising school leaders, and then supporting them as they plan and open new charter schools. Incubators provide these emerging school leaders with lots of technical assistance, mentoring, connections to board members, help in creating the vision for an excellent school, links to peer school leaders who can share strategies, assistance in getting authorized by local authorities, guidance in finding a facility, and support in securing launch funding from donors and then per-pupil public funding. School incubator organizations like the Mind Trust in Indianapolis, New Schools for New Orleans, Get Smart Schools in Denver, Charter School Partners in Minneapolis, and the Tennessee Charter School Incubator pull disparate resources into one place and dramatically improve the odds that a new school startup will succeed—both with students and in the practical demands of operation.

Growth accelerators are relatively new. Their goal is to ensure that leaders of existing individual charter schools or networks that are performing well have the support they need to replicate themselves. In early 2014 three excellent charter networks—Achievement First, YES Prep, and Aspire Public Schools—launched the Charter Network Accelerator. It offers twice-a-month sessions on designing, building, and managing an expanding stable of schools. This includes assistance on finding good teachers and principals, advice on management structure, and curriculum and academic programming.

Choose to Succeed is another organization working to accelerate the growth of high-performing charters. Its strategy has been to recruit the nation's finest school operators to San Antonio, Texas, by providing grants directly to schools. It also supports broader efforts to expand parental choice and create an environment that fosters education innovation.

Harbormasters are typically foundations or nonprofits that operate citywide, advising many different schools on ways to increase the number of high-performing seats in the city. They provide vision, strategy, resources, talent, and political will to lead their community toward more great schools. Harbormasters often function as incubators and/or accelerators, but they generally play a much larger role. Education Cities, an umbrella group for harbormasters, identifies four main tasks: supporting quality schools, strengthening pipelines that produce effective teachers, advocating for useful policy changes, and building broad community support. Because of their deep community ties, knowledge of their cities, and ability to financially support projects, foundations can be highly effective harbormasters. Donors should, however, be aware that since harbormasters lead a specific type of long-term agenda, they function on—not below—the radar screen. So they must be prepared for public praise and public criticism alike.

Such organizations are often important in drawing the attention of top national organizations like Teach For America, New Leaders, Building Excellent Schools, and TNTP to their city. Some of these already partner with Catholic schools, and all of them have shown gifts for drawing unusually talented people into school reform. Harbormasters serve as a clearinghouse for information, a linker of schools and leaders, a cheerleader, a defender. Examples of harbormasters include the Mind Trust in Indianapolis, New Schools for New Orleans, Excellent Schools Detroit, Schools That Can Milwaukee, CityBridge Foundation in D.C., the Donnell-Kay Foundation in Denver, the Philadelphia School Partnership, and Accelerate Great Schools in Cincinnati.

To get a sense of how an organizing effort that includes Catholic schools in an ambitious citywide school reform push might unfold, let's look at the examples of the Philadelphia School Partnership and the Accelerate Great Schools coalition in Cincinnati. Both are "three-sector" efforts that deal evenhandedly with schools of different types. Both rely on hard performance measures to decide which schools to support. Both are focused on expansion of the schools that work.

Philadelphia School Partnership

Formed in 2011 by local business leader Mike O'Neill, a longtime supporter of Catholic and charter schools, the Philadelphia School Partnership is a nonprofit that raises philanthropic funds to increase the number of high-quality school seats in the city. And in the spirit of brotherly love, PSP is "sector-agnostic"—it will fund district-run, charter, or Catholic schools. Any operation that can show good results from students is eligible for expansion support.

The Partnership's goal is to raise $100 million by 2016 and create 35,000 new high-quality seats. It has already launched 15,800 additional high-quality seats after raising $65 million in donations from more than 50 individuals, corporations, and foundations. Lead investors offering $5 million or more include Janine and Jeff Yass, the Maguire Foundation, the Walton Family Foundation, and the William Penn Foundation.

To date, 55 percent of PSP funds have been invested in charter schools, 35 percent in district-run schools, and 10 percent in religious or private schools. Its Catholic-school beneficiaries include Cristo Rey Philadelphia High School, DePaul (a school in the Independence Mission School network using the Seton blended-learning model), St. Thomas Aquinas School (another IMS school), and Neumann-Goretti High School (part of the Faith in the Future network).

"New public schools cost $50 million, while Catholic schools cost taxpayers nothing. They're an unbelievable bargain for the city. And we lose some of our best seats when Catholic schools close. So we needed to find ways to work collaboratively," states Mike O'Neill.

PSP is intently focused on student outcomes. It expects students attending its schools to outperform Pennsylvania and the School District of Philadelphia averages and score similarly to high-performing schools in the city's suburbs. Early data show that approximately 70 percent of their investments are on track to meet or exceed their performance benchmarks, 17 percent are within reach, and only 13 percent are at risk of not meeting performance standards.

The Philadelphia School Partnership invests not just in schools but also in enabling organizations that help schools succeed. These include the PhillyPLUS program for training principals, the Great Philly Schools website that helps parents assess and compare schools, and the Great Schools Compact that the Gates Foundation funded to get conventional, charter, and religious/private schools cooperating on improving classroom results all across the city. They have also found it necessary to create sister advocacy and campaign-finance organizations to fend off school caps and hostile policies that could block the success of their nonprofit work.

Accelerate Great Schools

State data revealed in 2014 that nearly half of the Cincinnati City School District's campuses—27 out of 55—were significantly underperforming.

The district met none of the state standards in reading or math in grades 3-6, and earned an F on all of its progress indicators. Cincinnati's charter schools were little better: Black students in poverty who attended a charter school in Cincinnati slightly outperformed their peers in district-run schools in reading, but performed worse in math.

While less achievement data is available for Cincinnati's Catholic schools, Iowa test scores suggest that the average student in third through seventh grade at a Catholic school is at least one full year above grade level. Despite these good results, though, and the fact that Catholic schooling is mainstream in Cincinnati (enrolling nearly a quarter of the city's students at present), the business model of Catholic schools has been failing in Cincinnati as it has elsewhere: twenty-one schools there have been closed or consolidated over the past decade and enrollment is down nearly 20 percent since the 1996 school year.

Aiming to strengthen their city's entire portfolio of schools, including religious institutions, an impressive alliance of Cincinnati groups united in 2015 to form Accelerate Great Schools. The partners include local funders like the Farmer Family Foundation, the Haile/U.S. Bank Foundation, the Lovett and Ruth Peters Foundation, and the KnowledgeWorks Foundation, along with leaders from the city's business sector, and from the public, charter, and Catholic-school sector.

"It was important to get everyone to the table," explained Mary Beth Martin of the Farmer Family Foundation. "This required allaying some concerns. Some Catholic-school leaders, for example, were concerned that our fundraising might sap donations from their campaigns. But we assured them this is start-up money. It's additive."

The mission of Accelerate Great Schools is to double the number of seats available in excellent schools in the next five years, and then double it again five years after that, to a total of 20,000 new seats in high-performing district, charter, and religious or private schools. It will recruit school operators, build pipelines for teaching talent, engage the community, and advocate for policy improvements. To fund these activities Accelerate Great Schools set a goal of raising $25 million. Approximately $15 million will go toward creating new schools; $5 million will be used to attract organizations like Teach For America and New Leaders that train teachers; and the remaining $5 million will cover the organization's operations, including the community engagement and policy advocacy functions.

Asked what others interested in launching something similar in their hometown should know, Martin warns, "Stay true to the goal even when that means not everyone is happy. If you're really about transformation for the kids, this will involve some disruption, which upsets people. You need to be aware of the concerns that exist and you can allay some of those. But this is about creating change and not accepting the status quo."

Donors are the key to a Catholic-school renaissance
Methodical, nationwide growth of high-quality Catholic schools is likely to require the same deliberate investment in an infrastructure of incubators, accelerators, and harbormasters that fueled the rise of charter schools. Donors can be instrumental in either starting Catholic-school-specific counterparts to these organizations in their respective cities, or convincing existing organizations to fold Catholic schools into their services and strategies. For example, donors could supply the funding that allows an existing incubator to train and support a leader who would then work with local officials to open a new Catholic school in their city.

> Nationwide growth of high-quality Catholic schools is likely to require the same investment in incubators and accelerators that fueled the rise of charters.

New approaches that emphasize a citywide "system of schools" will necessarily include a sharp focus on continual improvement, marked by new entrants, systemwide comparisons, careful school shopping by parents, and a gradual raising of the bar of excellence. We've argued in this chapter that it will be extremely helpful to Catholic institutions if they are included as integral parts of their city's system of schools. But for that to happen they need to shift to a growth and constant-improvement mentality—raising student results, expanding good existing schools, opening new schools, closing consistently low-performing schools, and otherwise meeting community demand.

Donors should continue to support schools directly. They must continue to help students access existing schools through scholarships. They should consider new governance approaches and new school models. They should explore partnerships with universities and other pipelines of teachers and leaders. They should work to make public policies friendlier to Catholic schools. But donors should also think through how all of those streams might fit together and become mutually reinforcing in a wider citywide strategy.

Indeed, donors should be prepared to shift part of their support away from a geographic focus and look instead for the very best investment opportunities, regardless of where they're located, with one eye on serving the most children and another eye on creating successful models that can be copied elsewhere. Not all schools and dioceses are open to help, so finding a good investment may mean searching for leaders or entrepreneurs who are willing and ready to work with you on innovative projects, even if they're not nearby. In certain cases a new approach can be supported and honed elsewhere, and then imported back into your home region.

For centuries, Catholic schools have provided a high-quality education to children across the country. They are providing a particularly precious service to the nation today by educating millions of disadvantaged boys and girls from poor urban neighborhoods where families have miserable options in conventional schools. So it's urgent that solutions be found to the steep challenges that have closed so many Catholic schools over the last 50 years.

We are beginning to see the outlines of a systemic solution to this half-century problem. New approaches to school organization, governance, public policy, teaching talent, and other areas are combining to breathe new life into Catholic schooling. Much more than in other, more mature, philanthropic fields, donors have a tremendous opportunity today to make major differences in this area. Regardless of a philanthropist's giving preferences or experience or location, the avenues leading to a renaissance of Catholic schooling are wide open. There are hundreds of ways you can be part of the revitalization of this precious national asset.

APPENDIX

Other Sample Opportunities for Donors

Donors can offer the resources and creative force needed to reimagine, retool, and re-energize our storied Catholic schools. Exactly how you invest will depend on your interests and expertise, your objectives, your funding levels, and your risk tolerance. Fertile openings for donors have been mentioned throughout the preceding six chapters. As a stimulus to action, we list in this Appendix some further sample ideas of investment opportunities. These emerge from our recent work with leading Catholic-school philanthropists, high-achieving nonprofits, and top education reformers.

Investments under $50,000

- **Get grantees to share knowledge**
  Russ Carson, the New York-based philanthropist who supports Catholic and charter schools, recently sent Catholic-school leaders from the Partnership for Inner-city Education to the KIPP School Summit, the annual knowledge-sharing and culture-building gathering of the country's most successful charter-school chain. He was able to ask the two groups to work together because he gives to both KIPP and the Partnership.

- **Help schools reinforce their Catholicity**
  The aspect of Catholic schools that makes them attractive to many parents, of all religious backgrounds, is their strong moral education and faith formation. Catholic Education Honor Roll is a mechanism for making sure this central strength doesn't get watered down. It's an in-depth assessment and competition for schools that provides tools Catholic schools can use to see how they're doing on this aspect of school excellence.

- **Train school leaders to work with Hispanic families**
  Over 100 schools have participated in the University of Notre

Dame's four-day Latino Enrollment Institute. Enrollment at those schools has subsequently gone up an average of 18 percent. Donors should sponsor the attendance of willing schools.

- **Survey pastors to find those who want to be involved in bolstering schools**

  While some pastors don't like working with schools, or feel they don't have the time, there is no methodical research on this. One donor recently suggested, "Can't we just organize a survey of pastors to find the ones who want to pour themselves into schooling?"

- **Help new priests get involved with schools**

  New York's Catholic Education Foundation has started offering seminars for new priests and seminarians on how to build strong relationships with parish schools. The School Pastors' Institute at the University of Notre Dame also offers a workshop on how priests can be effective at parish schools, with instruction on working with boards, on budgeting, on how to build a strong relationship with a principal, on recruiting Latino families, and so forth.

Investments of $50,000–$250,000

- **Research public views of Catholic schools**

  Catholic schools can no longer assume the public knows about their good results, or even that they exist. Where members of the public have views, they are often fuzzy or inaccurate. Better understanding of what people think of Catholic schools is the first step toward making the schools responsive and attractive to potential customers and supporters. What do parents want from a Catholic school that they are willing to pay for? Is the "brand" of Catholic education still strong? Modern, professional research paid for by donors could provide valuable information on how better to reach families and engage with the public at large.

- **Help Catholic schools tell their story**

  One thing Catholic schools are not good at is promoting themselves. "We just don't do it," admits the Reverend Brendan McGuire of the Diocese of San Jose. "Money is almost always better spent on direct services. But philanthropists can help us treat telling our story as an investment." Entrepreneur and philanthropist Mike O'Neill agrees that Catholic schools "need to stand up and profess their excellence. Say what our schools are doing for our state and nation." Consider creating a communications organization devoted to Catholic school issues. Distribute statistics and research. Help schools design events that will attract reporters. Catholic schools are rarely discussed in regional and national media at present.

- **Encourage a growth mindset**
  It's estimated that half of all new seats in American schools over the next ten years will be created by operators that don't yet exist. Catholic schools need to participate in that process of invention, and donors should press for fresh thinking along those lines. We can't assume yesterday's Catholic schools or support organizations will fit into future needs. The Catholic school sector has few of the legal and bureaucratic constraints that can keep district or charter schools from imaginative expansion. But innovation has not been a strong suit of Catholic-school leaders over the last generation, and donors could help spur creativity by hosting school-design competitions and business-plan contests.

- **Improve development and enrollment infrastructure**
  The Healey Education Foundation helps clusters of schools professionalize their fundraising functions. It pays for intensive professional training that moves schools beyond the bingo-and-candy-bars culture into annual appeals that can reliably raise six-figures. Six schools can go through the Healey program for about $200,000 per year (part of which funds development directors for the schools).

- **Help retain excellent specialized teachers**
  When schools encounter financial hardships, it's easy to cut honors-level teachers, who tend to be comparatively expensive because they focus just on top students. In Philadelphia, the Connelly Foundation has helped schools share great honors teachers via high-definition video conferencing that lets a particular advanced-math instructor, for instance, reach kids at multiple

schools. "Kids love it, and we're saving schools a ton of money," according to Connelly's Kim Flaville. This is a way to keep physics, Latin, AP history, and other honors classes in Catholic education.

- **Study the inner-city Catholic-school model to extract the patterns of successful institutions**
  Why are some urban Catholic schools so much more successful than others? Which positive traits do good schools have in common? What do they fuss over and what do they skip? The research to answer those basic questions doesn't exist—though it would be invaluable to schools trying to direct limited resources, especially in locations without publicly funded school choice. Donors could solve that.

- **Insist on real, accurate statistics**
  In New York City, Catholic schools regularly claimed that 99 percent of their students graduated from high school. "It didn't seem plausible to me that 99 percent of the kids who started in Catholic high school were in fact graduating four years later. No school of any type pulls that off," explains donor Russ Carson. "Sure enough, when we began to look more closely, the numbers proved closer to 80 percent. That, by the way, is a fantastic statistic for this population. But we as donors should continue to probe and ask for a high level of accountability from the system." Other crucial measures can be equally foggy, which is not helpful to students, to the cause of school improvement, or to marketing efforts. In Los Angeles, donors were able to obtain solid performance measures after engaging with school officials. In other places as well, donors need to explain how data transparency will help Catholic schools over the long-term, and work with schools on accurately gathering and sharing numbers.

- **Attract nontraditional candidates to work in Catholic schools**
  "The biggest collective 'donation' to Catholic education comes from Catholic school teachers and principals—many of whom could earn $20,000 to $30,000 more each year at public or charter schools," says Leo Linbeck. "They're foregoing pay to serve a higher purpose." Many of these teachers find Catholic schools, instead of the reverse. Donors can play a valuable role in helping schools develop better ways to attract, train, pay, and

retain effective educators who are drawn to the mission of these schools. Since Catholic schools typically don't have the same credential mandates and union demands as public schools, there is opportunity to recruit content experts and other impressive but non-conventional educators from the ranks of recent retirees, at-home parents returning to work, or community members interested in teaching specialized classes part time.

Investments of $250,000–$1 million

- **Expand Catholic early education**
  Preschool programs are increasingly the pipelines that feed students to elementary schools. And in many states there are public-funding options that will pay for pre-K programming, including by religious and private operators. Donors might boost Catholic early education by investing in excellent preschool teacher training.

- **Fund incentives to fill remaining seats**
  There's debate about what should be done with the last remaining seats in a school. The Reverend Joe Corpora from Notre Dame's Catholic School Advantage program thinks it's essential for Catholic schools to be full. "The best form of development is a butt in a seat," he argues. Agreeing, Pennsylvania businessman and philanthropist Mark Lieberman decided to fund a pilot in Allentown. With his support, Catholic schools began offering tuition discounts to students who transferred from public, charter, non-Catholic private, or home schools. Tuition was discounted $2,000 during the first year, and $1,000 the second year. Schools received a $4,000 advertising budget to spread the word, and were themselves offered a $300 incentive for each transferee they enrolled. The first year, the diocese filled 448 previously empty seats across 38 schools, reversing a 15-year enrollment decline and making the diocese the only Northeast Catholic school system to increase enrollment. Fully 95 percent of the transfers remained in Catholic schools after three years. An additional $3.5 million in annual revenue was generated by the program, so it more than paid for itself. "Schools need to understand that not everyone needs to pay the same amount," Lieberman says, noting that businesses use selective discounting all the time to reach optimal market penetration.

- **Pull Catholic schools into citywide education reforms**
  Catholic schools can participate in citywide school application systems like New Orleans' OneApp. They can share data through transparency sites like GreatSchools.org. They can participate in cross-sector leadership-training programs like PhillyPLUS. Donors should push, and help, Catholic schools to connect with citywide organizations that bolster excellent schools of all sorts. Venture funds looking to support great schools are likewise increasingly willing to include Catholic institutions. But Catholic schools need to position themselves better by building top-notch operational processes, transparent metrics, and proven leaders. If donors can get Catholic-school leaders rubbing elbows with school-reform leaders, all those improvements will be speeded.

- **Help parents and community neighbors advocate for school-choice policies**
  School-choice expansions can benefit Catholic schools enormously, yet they are rarely driven or aggressively supported by school leaders or stakeholders. Backers need to help Catholic schools become active in policy debates and grassroots advocacy like their charter-school cousins have. Participation in rallies supporting beneficial legislation, protests of unfair practices, and public meetings where important information is shared are valuable. Donors can help activate the roughly 2 million Catholic-school families nationwide into a group with a voice and political presence.

- **Offer top teachers incentives to stay in the classroom**
  Talented young teachers right out of college or an alternative teacher-prep program often stay only a couple years. Donors eager to retain top talent are finding that offering retention bonuses at the end of their initial two-year commitment can turn many of these individuals into longer-term teachers. Tiered bonuses, mentoring, and other incentives, which are not particularly expensive, also show promise.

- **Pay for excellent consultants**
  Today's education reform movement is producing some wonderful nonprofits that provide sharp, savvy consulting advice proven to work in various settings. This is one of the hardest things for any Catholic

school to get into its budget, but it can be very useful. One excellent option is EdPioneers, a group founded by a former teacher in Notre Dame's ACE program. EdPioneers places graduate students and young professionals with business, education, law, or policy expertise in consulting roles at schools, where they dispense fresh insights at a fraction of the cost of traditional consulting companies.

Investments of $1 million or more

- **Build a leadership program for cultivating talent**
  Leadership openings in Catholic schools are often met with scurrying and panic, without confidence that talented candidates have already been groomed for responsibility. Developing a prestigious fellowship program that trains talented, faith-filled individuals to be principals in inner-city Catholic schools—along the lines of the programs funded by the Broad Foundation for public-school leaders—could be helpful.

- **Start new independent organizations like Seton Partners, ACE, Healey, and the Drexel Fund**
  It took the charter sector two decades to build up its robust network of support organizations. Catholic schooling has recently developed some stars of its own but it lacks an ecosystem of adequate capacity and richness to support the thousands of schools and millions of children already in Catholic education, and the many more who could be attracted in a growth environment. "We need to try experimenting with new ideas," argues Leo Linbeck. "Unproven seed work can have a significant failure rate, but early stage experiments don't cost as much as bailing out a system later, and new ideas may unlock some ways to save schools."

- **Create an Urban Catholic Teacher Corps**
  The Match Teacher Residency in Boston gathers candidates hoping to become charter-school teachers, houses them together, provides intensive training, and teaching experience at a superb school, crowned by a master's degree at the end. Yet the price is far lower than a university teaching credential. This model would not be hard to copy, and it could help draw top talent from the still largely untapped Catholic-college market into teaching.

- **Focus some initial efforts on a few opportune cities**
  The nation's savviest Catholic donors should make sure they overlap and concentrate some of their interventions on particular cities—so that school success becomes obvious in that location, generates excitement, and can then be exported as a proven commodity. A few compelling examples of what's possible when serious attention is given to Catholic schooling could be highly influential and inspirational.

- **Expand Catholic "wraparound" programs at charter schools**
  Wraparound services provided before or after school or during lunch breaks allow students at public schools to get religious training and mentoring on a voluntary basis. Groups like Education Enterprises, Catalyst Schools, and others are starting to provide these services for charters. These offer moral and spiritual education to students not in Catholic schools, and they create critical connections that might help soften the sometimes silly and unnecessary divisions between religious and secular education, and pave the way for fairer treatment of religious schools when reimbursements are made for educating children. A group that specialized in bringing these services to existing charters could be very helpful.

- **Explore opportunities for locating charter schools in church buildings**
  Instead of closing down Catholic schools entirely where they are not financially viable, the church might cooperate in the establishment of charter schools in their school buildings, perhaps with "wraparound" services as described above. This can soften disruptions of students, offer new opportunities for faith formation, and offer productive use of real-estate assets that could otherwise become burdens on the community and the church.

- **Expect national education-reform programs to work with Catholic schools**
  Don't restrict your search for third-party providers to known Catholic school organizations. Look for the best minds and deepest experience to tackle a particular need and then ask the service provider to consider working with Catholic schools, with

your support. Organizations like Teach For America, EdPioneers, Building Excellent Schools, and New Leaders should be funded specifically to expand the number Catholic educators coming through their programs.

- **Create a national Catholic-school movement for data transparency and consistent metrics**
  Despite a generally strong reputation for academic success, Catholic schools are poor at providing performance data. Sometimes the problem is as simple as an overtaxed principal not finding time to create annual reports. Sometimes a school would rather just trade on its reputation—usually self-defined—than submit to external scrutiny. Donors can help ensure there is accurate, open, consistent measurement of crucial indicators of student performance and school finances by helping schools gather, present, and share key data. This will in turn promote a culture of continuous improvement.

INDEX

ABOUT THE PHILANTHROPY ROUNDTABLE

The Philanthropy Roundtable is America's leading network of charitable donors working to strengthen our free society, uphold donor intent, and protect the freedom to give. Our members include individual philanthropists, families, corporations, and private foundations.

Mission

The Philanthropy Roundtable's mission is to foster excellence in philanthropy, to protect philanthropic freedom, to assist donors in achieving their philanthropic intent, and to help donors advance liberty, opportunity, and personal responsibility in America and abroad.

Principles

- Philanthropic freedom is essential to a free society
- A vibrant private sector generates the wealth that makes philanthropy possible
- Voluntary private action offers solutions to many of society's most pressing challenges
- Excellence in philanthropy is measured by results, not by good intentions
- A respect for donor intent is essential to long-term philanthropic success

Services

World-class conferences

The Philanthropy Roundtable connects you with other savvy donors. Held across the nation throughout the year, our meetings assemble grantmakers and experts to develop strategies for excellent local, state, and national giving. You will hear from innovators in K–12 education, economic opportunity, higher education, national security, and other fields. Our Annual Meeting is the Roundtable's flagship event, gathering the nation's most public-spirited and influential philanthropists for debates, how-to sessions, and discussions on the best ways for private individuals to achieve powerful results through their giving. The Annual Meeting is a stimulating and enjoyable way to meet principled donors seeking the breakthroughs that can solve our nation's greatest challenges.

Breakthrough groups
Our Breakthrough groups—focused program areas—build a critical mass of donors around a topic where dramatic results are within reach. Breakthrough groups become a springboard to help donors achieve lasting effects from their philanthropy. Our specialized staff of experts helps grantmakers invest with care in areas like anti-poverty work, philanthropy for veterans, and family reinforcement. The Roundtable's K–12 education program is our largest and longest-running Breakthrough group. This network helps donors zero in on today's most promising school reforms. We are the industry-leading convener for philanthropists seeking systemic improvements through competition and parental choice, administrative freedom and accountability, student-centered technology, enhanced teaching and school leadership, and high standards and expectations for students of all backgrounds. We foster productive collaboration among donors of varied ideological perspectives who are united by a devotion to educational excellence.

A powerful voice
The Roundtable's public-policy project, the Alliance for Charitable Reform (ACR), works to advance the principles and preserve the rights of private giving. ACR educates legislators and policymakers about the central role of charitable giving in American life and the crucial importance of protecting philanthropic freedom—the ability of individuals and private organizations to determine how and where to direct their charitable assets. Active in Washington, D.C., and in the states, ACR protects charitable giving, defends the diversity of charitable causes, and battles intrusive government regulation. We believe the capacity of private initiative to address national problems must not be burdened with costly or crippling constraints.

Protection of donor interests
The Philanthropy Roundtable is the leading force in American philanthropy to protect donor intent. Generous givers want assurance that their money will be used for the specific charitable aims and purposes they

believe in, not redirected to some other agenda. Unfortunately, donor intent is usually violated in increments, as foundation staff and trustees neglect or misconstrue the founder's values and drift into other purposes. Through education, practical guidance, legislative action, and individual consultation. The Philanthropy Roundtable is active in guarding donor intent. We are happy to advise you on steps you can take to ensure that your mission and goals are protected.

Must-read publications

Philanthropy, the Roundtable's quarterly magazine, is packed with useful and beautifully written real-life stories. It offers practical examples, inspiration, detailed information, history, and clear guidance on the differences between giving that is great and giving that disappoints. We also publish a series of guidebooks that provide detailed information on the very best ways to be effective in particular aspects of philanthropy. These guidebooks are compact, brisk, and readable. Most focus on one particular area of giving—for instance, how to improve teaching, charter school expansion, support for veterans, programs that get the poor into jobs, how to invest in public policy, and other topics of interest to grantmakers. Real-life examples, hard numbers, first-hand experiences of other donors, recent history, and policy guidance are presented to inform and inspire savvy donors.

Join the Roundtable!

When working with The Philanthropy Roundtable, members are better equipped to achieve long-lasting success with their charitable giving. Your membership in the Roundtable will make you part of a potent network that understands philanthropy and strengthens our free society. Philanthropy Roundtable members range from Forbes 400 individual givers and the largest American foundations to small family foundations and donors just beginning their charitable careers. Our members include:

- Individuals and families
- Private foundations
- Community foundations
- Venture philanthropists
- Corporate giving programs
- Large operating foundations and charities that devote more than half of their budget to external grants

Philanthropists who contribute at least $100,000 annually to charitable causes are eligible to become members of the Roundtable and register for most of our programs. Roundtable events provide you with a solicitation-free environment.

For more information on The Philanthropy Roundtable or to learn about our individual program areas, please call (202) 822-8333 or e-mail main@PhilanthropyRoundtable.org.

ABOUT THE AUTHORS

Andy Smarick is author of the Roundtable guidebook *Closing America's High-achievement Gap: A Wise Giver's Guide to Helping Our Most Talented Students*. He is also author of *The Urban School System of the Future*, and currently advises on all aspects of school management at Bellwether Education Partners. He previously served as New Jersey's Deputy Commissioner of Education, as Deputy Assistant Secretary at the U.S. Department of Education, and on the White House Domestic Policy Council. He is a member of the Maryland State Board of Education.

Kelly Robson analyzes policy at Bellwether Education Partners. She previously taught middle school in Ohio and Washington, D.C., and helped create school curricula in D.C. She holds bachelor's and master's degrees from Ohio State University, and is pursuing a doctorate in education policy at George Washington University.